ALSO BY JAMES BEARD

Hors d'Oeuvre and Canapés

Cook It Outdoors

Fowl and Game Cookery

The Fireside Cookbook

Paris Cuisine
(with Alexander Watt)

Jim Beard's New Barbecue Cookbook

James Beard's New Fish Cookery

The Complete Book of Outdoor Cookery
(with Helen Evans Brown)

How to Eat Better for Less Money
(with Sam Aaron)

The James Beard Cookbook

James Beard's Treasury of Outdoor Cooking

Delights and Prejudices

Menus for Entertaining

How to Eat (and Drink) Your Way
Through a French (or Italian) Menu

James Beard's American Cookery

Beard on Food

Theory & Practice of Good Cooking

The New James Beard

Beard on Pasta

BEARD ON BREAD

Drawings by Karl Stuecklen

1996 / ALFRED A. KNOPF / New York

Beard
ON BREAD

by
James Beard

*With an Introduction by Chuck Williams
for the 1995 edition*

This Is a Borzoi Book
Published by Alfred A. Knopf, Inc.

Grateful acknowledgment is made to the following for permission to reprint previously published material:

Atheneum Publishers and George Lang: Recipe for George Lang's Potato Bread with Caraway Seeds from *The Cuisine of Hungary*, by George Lang. Copyright © 1971 by George Lang.

Alfred A. Knopf, Inc.: Recipe for Jane Grigson's Walnut Bread from Southern Burgundy from *Good Things*, by Jane Grigson. Copyright © 1968, 1969, 1970, 1971, by Jane Grigson. Copyright © 1971 by Alfred A. Knopf, Inc.

The New York Times: Recipe for Finnish Sour Rye Bread and recipe for Sourdough Rye Bread. Copyright © 1968 by The New York Times. Reprinted by permission.

Random House, Inc.: Recipe for Pizza Caccia Nanza from *Italian Family Cooking*, by Edward Giobbi. Copyright © 1971 by Edward Giobbi.

Library of Congress Cataloging-in-Publication Data
Beard, James Andrew, 1903–1984
Beard on bread.
1. Bread. I. Title.
TX769.B33 1973 641.8'15 73–7266
ISBN 0-394-47345-0
ISBN 0-679-75504-7 (pbk.)

Manufactured in the United States of America

Published October 23, 1973
First Trade Paperback Edition, February 1995
Reprinted Once
Third Printing, March 1996

This book is dedicated to
ELIZABETH DAVID,
who loves bread

I am grateful to the following people who helped to test and
retest the recipes which appear in this book:

John Ferrone
Neil Micucci
Pearl Bresev
Janet Wurtzburger
Emil Kashouty
Eleanor Noderer
Tina Cassell
Felipe Rojas-Lombardi

And at least twenty others who were eager to test the recipes.

Contents

Introduction

Jim, as James Beard was known to his many friends, loved to make bread. He loved the feel of the dough against his hands, and, as he often expressed, "You really can't make good bread unless you can feel the texture, softness, and elasticity of the dough through your hands." Ask him how long to knead the dough and the answer would probably be: Until it feels right!

Jim was an imposing sight standing at a table with a mound of dough in front of him, his large hands caressing the dough, turning and folding it, until just the right moment, when he would stop, poke it with a finger, and pronounce it ready for rising.

During the months and months this book was in its formative stages, bread was an all-consuming interest for him. It was a rebellion against the lifeless and characterless bread found on the shelves of the American supermarket. America had developed the automobile, the airplane, and the refrigerator, and had won the wars, but had failed miserably at making bread. Soft, spongy pre-sliced white bread with little flavor, slathered with butter or margarine and topped with peanut butter or jam, was what America was eating. There was little objection from most people, but Jim thought differently and was on a crusade to correct this sad state of breadmaking.

I remember Jim in his New York kitchen kneading yet another version of sourdough bread with the hope of replicating the crusty sourdough of San Francisco's North Beach. I remember him in my kitchen in San Francisco trying out a buttermilk honey bread. It was a time for experimenting with new flours from small mills, new and stronger yeasts, putting tiles and pans of water in the oven to create steam—all in the quest to duplicate the crusty loaves of France. Jim had great and lengthy discussions on why the bread in France was so crusty and delicious. Was it the yeast? Was it the brick ovens in the basements of those charming Parisian bakeries? As I remember, the final consensus of opinion from Jim, Elizabeth David, and others was that it was the flour. Yes, the flour—French flour was different! Yet, how different? Elizabeth David's final pronouncement on the whole dilemma was, "You cannot duplicate it. You do not have the French flour and you are not in France, so there is really no reason to discuss it further." But Jim was never one to dismiss a challenge. He continued with his experiments and his discussions on how the best of European breads could be reproduced on this side of the Atlantic. Of course he was right. Now there are excellent European-type breads baked in this country.

After its publication in the autumn of 1973, *Beard on Bread* accomplished what Jim had in mind—encouraging home cooks to bake bread. And bake bread they did! Not only that, they became more interested in taking cooking lessons. Also at this time, a new breed of chef was in its formative years—the Young American Chef! These young American chefs, fresh from a cooking school or culinary academy, emerged eager to change the way we ate. They wanted better bread in their restaurants, so they began baking their own crusty loaves. Some of the young bakers getting their first chance at creating these breads in the latest "in" restaurants soon started their own small bakeries, baking crusty country loaves of French and Italian origin.

With the increased interest in breadmaking, new flours appeared on the market—unbleached bread flours, hard-wheat flours, stoneground flours. Also new, improved active dry yeasts—stronger yeasts, faster-acting yeasts, most of them meant to be simply added to the flour. Some dedicated bakers would disdain commercial yeast, developing methods for capturing wild yeast to create "starters." The shelves of the ubiquitous soft white sliced breads began to shrink while more interesting country-type loaves began to appear.

Today there are even more inducements for making your own bread. As well as the faster-acting yeasts, now there is a wheat gluten flour on the market that increases the gluten content of regular flour for better rising. New bread boosters, also containing wheat gluten as well as malt, will make your doughs rise more and give home-baked loaves the delicious malt flavor that we love in good crusty country breads. The electric bread machine, developed in Japan, has been a big hit with bread-loving Americans from the moment it was introduced here. The idea of fresh warm bread produced in your own home at a preset time and with little effort has great appeal, especially among people not particularly interested in cooking. Jim would have been fascinated with the machine, as he was with the food processor when it first appeared, and would have experimented at great length with it. I am sure that his final appraisal of the machine would be that it has a rightful place in the homes of people too busy to bake or really not interested in baking, but that it cannot replace "hands-on" breadmaking any more than machine-made pies have equaled handmade ones. Unfortunately it will not produce, on its own, the crusty country loaves I have been talking about. If you want to understand the art of bread baking, get your hands in the dough.

Even though breadmaking has changed considerably since the publication of *Beard on Bread*, the book is as viable today as it was in 1973. With its simple instructions and easy-to-follow recipes, new dimensions in breadmaking have been created for the home cook. To quote Jim: "I find it always pleasant at the beginning of a day to "proof" the yeast, to plunge my hands into the dough and bring it to life, to watch it rise, and to wait for the moment when the finished loaf can be taken from the oven. There is no smell in the world of food to equal the perfume of baking bread and few greater pleasures in eating than sitting down with a slice of freshly baked bread, good butter, and a cup of tea or coffee." I heartily agree!

Chuck Williams

OBSERVATIONS

Flour

To make yeast bread we need wheat flour, which contains a protein called "gluten." When we stir and knead dough, gluten is the ingredient that makes the elasticity, holds in the gas caused by the fermenting yeast, and creates the architectural plan of the bread. The flour called "all-purpose," which is the most generally available flour, is wheat flour. It comes both bleached and unbleached, and because it is a sturdier flour and has better texture, the unbleached is preferable. Unbleached flour has long been available from Standard Mills under two brand names, and it is interesting to note that the larger mills, like Pillsbury, General Mills, and Robin Hood, who up until this time have promoted bleached flour, with its "enrichments," are also beginning to offer unbleached flour, as well as flours that are much more vigorous, such as coarsely ground meals. This is a great advance in the world of commercial foods, one that I am sure is motivated by the tremendous interest in stone-ground flours and special flours turned out by small mills across the country in the last five or six years now that breadmaking has become a popular art again. People will even go right to the source to buy these flours, or buy them in specialty health food shops.

While I have used all-purpose flour extensively in testing recipes for this book, it is not the best flour to use for making breads. The choicest kind is the hard-wheat flour used by professional bakers, and if you have a cooperative bakery in your neighborhood you might ask if you can buy some. You can also buy hard-wheat flours from some health food stores or by mail order—some made from North Dakota hard wheat, some from Texas hard wheat. Any of them will make a beautiful, firm-crumbed bread, a bread that will elicit compliments from practically everyone who tastes it.

There is no standardization of flours from one brand to another or from one part of the country to another to help the breadmaker produce uniform loaves of bread, although at one time General Mills offered an all-purpose flour that was considered to be standard throughout the country. I am afraid that this is no longer the case, so one can safely say there are no two flours on the market that really react alike.

As I will mention many times throughout this book, it is almost im-

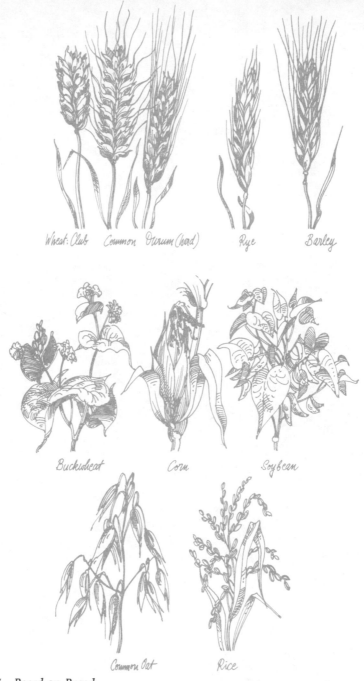

Wheat: Club Common Durum (head) Rye Barley

Buckwheat Corn Soybean

Common Oat Rice

possible to give an exact amount of flour for each recipe because of the difference in the characteristics of flour, as well as variations in the atmosphere. Therefore when a recipe calls for kneading in extra flour, you may require more than I suggest. If this happens, do not be alarmed. Go ahead, add flour, and try to achieve a dough that has a good consistency. Eventually your hands will learn when you have reached the right amount of flour and the right degree of kneading.

If you become a serious breadmaker, you will want to play with various special flours, like graham or barley flour. There are also meals and components of the grain you can use, but these are strictly additives; they cannot be used alone to make bread, since they do not react to yeast and must therefore be combined with wheat flour. The veteran breadmaker is always on the lookout for special flours and additives, and if you search your city or countryside you may discover some new varieties for yourself.

Special Flours, Meals, and Additives

Meals are coarsely ground grains, a number of which are used extensively in breadmaking. The best known of these is oatmeal, also known as steel-cut oatmeal, and rolled oats—that is, oats that are rolled into a very coarse meal, giving them an entirely different texture from the whole grain.

Barley meal, which is a coarsely ground version of the whole kernel of barley, is called for in a few recipes. Barley flour, a finer milling of the kernel, is used in combination with wheat flour in some breads.

Whole-wheat flour is different in texture from whole-meal flour or whole-wheat meal; the latter two are much more coarsely ground and contain rough bits of bran and crushed kernels.

Rye meal should be differentiated from rye flour in much the same way; it is coarse, rough, and bakes into a more crunchy loaf.

Bran is found in whole-wheat flour and whole-wheat meal and is also sold by itself. It is very coarse and has little to offer save its texture.

Graham flour is a ground whole-wheat grain that includes the bran. It was developed by Dr. Sylvester Graham.

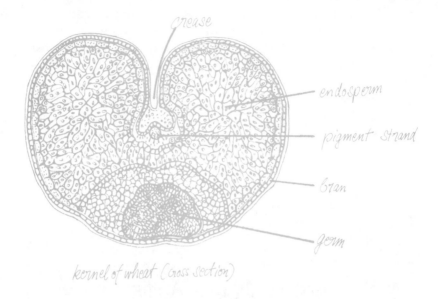

crease
endosperm
pigment strand
bran
germ

kernel of wheat (cross section)

Gluten is the protein component of grain. Gluten flour has had practically all starch removed and is used widely in diatetic breads.

The wheat germ is the sprouting section of the seed and is often removed from flours because it contains fat, which limits the keeping qualities of bread. But it is full of nutrients and today it is available separately and is much used as a cereal, as an additive to breads, and as animal food.

Whole-wheat kernels or whole-wheat berries are the whole kernels of wheat, which contain the bran, the germ, the gluten—everything. Some people like it whole in breads to add texture (it must be cooked first); it can also be eaten as a cereal, or you can grind it to use as a meal.

Cracked wheat is coarsely ground whole wheat, which is commonly used as a cereal; it adds a crunchy taste and nutty flavor to breads.

Buckwheat was originally known as beechwheat because of its triangular seed. It is native to Russia and was brought to Europe during the Crusades. It is used principally for buckwheat cakes, for blini, and sometimes as a cereal. Buckwheat can be ground—in fact, it is one of the few grains that can be ground in a blender.

Stone-ground flour is flour that has been milled by stone rollers, which are very often propelled by water power. Many people feel that this method of grinding produces a more nutritious and honest flour than modern milled flour. It is apt to be coarser and heavier, and you will find that you need to use about double the amount of yeast when you are making bread with stone-ground flour.

Hard-wheat flour is usually made from spring wheat, particularly that from the West, Middle West, and Southwest, and notably from Deafsmith County in Texas. Hard-wheat flours are noted for their mineral content and for making firm, rather elastic breads. In England it is called "strong flour."

Soft-wheat flour in this country comes mostly from the Midwest and is noted for its smoothness, which is an asset in making pastries and cakes.

Soybean flour is finely ground soybeans; it may be added to other flours in baking. It is an enrichment rather than a flour, and has a low fat content.

Brown rice when milled produces a heavy, dark flour called rice flour, which has a very rich flavor and gives a heavy character to anything to which it is added.

Leavening

A number of leavening agents are used in breadmaking, but the most common is yeast, in either compressed or active dry form.

Compressed or fresh yeast, as it is sometimes called, is sold in cakes in three sizes—a little over one-half ounce, one ounce, and two ounces—and also in quarter-pound and one-pound packages. It can be kept in the refrigerator for about ten to fourteen days; it can also be frozen successfully, but it must be defrosted at room temperature and used immediately. If you buy a large package of yeast, it is wise to cut it into one-batch pieces and freeze them separately.

Active dry yeast has replaced compressed yeast in most parts of the country. It is most commonly available in individual packets, containing approximately a tablespoon, and it can also sometimes be found in four-ounce jars. The yeast in a small package has the expiration date marked on the outside, but if you buy it in larger bulk in health food stores, the packages aren't apt to be dated and you should "proof" the yeast before using, as described on page 23. If you buy yeast in larger quantities, measure 1 scant tablespoon to equal 1 package of active dry yeast or a half-ounce cake of compressed yeast.

Active dry yeast should be dissolved in liquid at a temperature of about 100° to 115°, while compressed yeast should be dissolved in liquid that is no warmer than about 95°. These limits should be carefully observed. The first few times you make bread, you should take the temperature of the water with a thermometer, noting how warm it feels on your wrist when it is at the proper degree. After that you can gauge the temperature accurately enough just by the feel.

There is a new method being promoted today whereby dried yeast is simply blended with the other dry ingredients and then mixed with liquid that has been heated to as much as 120° to 130°. A lot of people like this method because it is so easy. Frankly, I find that while it may cut down your time, I prefer the old-fashioned way; perhaps the dough rises faster, but it is at the expense of the final flavor, it seems to me.

For yeast to become activated—that is, to release the gas that causes dough to rise—it must have something to feed on. Give it a little sugar and the yeast cells are encouraged to go to work; thus when a sweetener is called for in a bread recipe, it is not serving simply as a flavor. Granulated sugar is most often used, but molasses, brown sugar, and honey are also common sweeteners. Salt, on the other hand, is used to slow the action of yeast, as well as to bring out the flavor of the bread.

Sourdough and salt-rising starters are homemade leavening agents, both very unpredictable. You can get better results if you use yeast as well, and your bread will be lighter and have more flavor—but that is something you can decide for yourself. Baking powder is another leavening agent; baking powder breads are extremely popular, and include many of the fruit and vegetable breads, such as zucchini bread and banana bread. Baking soda is still another leavening agent, and is often used in breads containing fruit, to counteract the acid. It is also used along with yeast in recipes like English crumpets, to sweeten the batter. You will encounter all of these leavening agents during the course of this book.

Like other aspects of breadmaking, the time required for the rising of dough is extremely variable, depending on such factors as warmth of the room, the temperature and humidity of the day, the character of the yeast, the flour, and the kneading. I feel that to give definite rising times for each recipe only tends to make the beginner more nervous, particularly if it takes a longer or a shorter time than I specify. So, instead, I have indicated how much the dough should grow in bulk, and illustrations will aid you.

mixer with dough hook, paddle, whisk, etc.

The Electric Mixer

Some heavy-duty electric mixers, such as the Kitchen Aid and the Robot Coupe, come equipped with a dough hook that transforms them into kneading machines. They are quick, they save muscle, and they are efficient. You can use an electric mixer from the very start, first, after the yeast is dissolved, to stir in the flour and the liquids, and then, with the aid of the dough hook, to do the kneading. After the first rising, the bread is punched down and returned to the mixer, which does the additional kneading. Naturally, the dough hook will do a faster, more thorough job than you can do by hand. It is best to consult the recipe book that accompanies your mixer for suggested kneading times, although the experienced breadmaker can soon judge for himself, and if there is a little less or a little more kneading done than required, it does not matter.

I have used the electric mixer a great deal, but never for the entire kneading procedure. I rather enjoy taking the dough from the mixer and finishing it off by hand. It seems to me that it gives the bread a better texture, but this may be my imagination. I have many friends who would not dream of kneading by hand any longer now that they have a dough hook. The choice is up to you. If you enjoy the relaxing exercise of kneading and breaking down the mixture into a smooth, elastic dough, then the machine will never make up for that pleasure. It is, however, a great innovation and an undeniable time saver.

If the dough hook is operated according to the manufacturer's instructions, it can be used to prepare any of the yeast breads, as well as some of the baking-powder breads, in this book.

Bread Pans

The sizes of the bread pans given with the recipes are recommendations and are not to be followed slavishly if good sense tells you otherwise. Since the process of breadmaking is filled with variables, as I have said repeatedly, you could well end up with too much or too little dough for the pans I

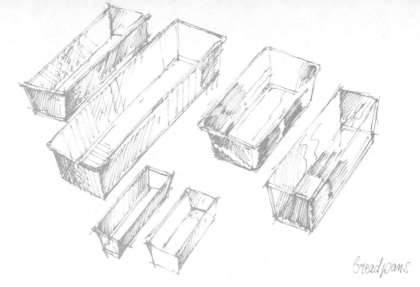

breadpans

have suggested. Therefore it is perhaps best to choose a pan after you have shaped a loaf, calculating how high the dough will be when it has doubled in bulk and allowing for a little extra rising during baking. Generally speaking, if you fill a loaf pan two-thirds full you will have a nicely arched loaf; if it is half full the loaf will be somewhat flatter in appearance.

Also, it is likely that many of you will not have access to the specialty shops that carry every shape and size bread pan, and you may well have to be content with the standard meat loaf pans found in most supermarkets. These, made of aluminum or of glass, are approximately 9¾ x 5¾ x 2¾ or 8½ x 4½ x 2½. You may find a couple of sizes in foil pans, too. Naturally you will have to adjust for these limitations, making one loaf where two might be called for, or two instead of one. With a little experimenting you will quickly be able to work out any pan problems.

tube pan

Greasing Bowls and Pans

You will note that practically every recipe for yeast bread calls for a buttered bowl in which the dough will be left to rise. This needs only a light buttering with a tablespoon or so—just enough to coat the dough with a thin film of fat when it is turned in the bowl, which is done to prevent it from drying out and developing a crust as it rises. I have specified using butter throughout the book, because that is my preference in most recipes. However, you can substitute margarine, oil, or any type of fat, even bacon fat. Beef drippings, goose fat, or chicken fat are also used for certain breads.

Pans can be buttered as lavishly or as sparingly as you like, as long as the inside surface is thoroughly coated. The average bread pan will take about 1 to 1½ tablespoons of butter. Again, you can use margarine, oil, any fat of your choice. Some people think that more fat makes a better loaf. That remains to be proved.

Cookie sheets are sometimes buttered (use approximately two tablespoons of fat); in other instances, a recipe will indicate that the sheet is merely sprinkled with cornmeal, some of which adheres to the loaf when baked. Teflon pans are not buttered.

Tiles

Several recipes in this book prescribe the use of tiles in the oven for baking bread, particularly when a definite crustiness is desired. The tiles I use are unglazed, brick-colored "quarry tiles" (check your telephone book for tile companies). I find that six tiles, each 5½ inches square, will line an oven rack neatly. The purpose of the tile is to produce a steady, evenly diffused heat, which is different from that radiated by the ordinary gas or electric oven. On the rack below, I generally install a pan of boiling water to create steam during the baking—it is the same technique used in baking French bread—which contributes to the crustiness of the bread. Most loaves baked in this way—rye, pumpernickel, "French-style," ordinary white—are done in loaf pans or on a baking sheet in the usual way,

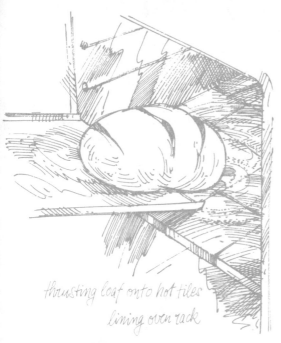

thrusting loaf onto hot tiles lining oven rack

but free-form loaves can be baked directly on the hot tiles sprinkled with cornmeal. Furthermore, there's no reason why you can't use tiles all the time, even when you are baking in a pan. When a loaf is just about done, remove it and tap it on the bottom to check (it will be done when it sounds hollow). Then place it directly on the preheated tiles for a final few minutes of baking, which will give a more interesting flavor and crust to the bread.

Cooling and Storing Bread

When you take bread from the oven, remove it from the pan, set it on a rack, and let it cool slowly, preferably in a draft-free place. When it is thoroughly cool place it in a plastic bag or plastic wrap, and refrigerate or store at room temperature. It will last from 2 to 7 days, depending on the character of the bread. If it is extremely moist watch carefully in case it should start to mold, although it very seldom does. If some mold has formed it can be cut away and the bread used without hesitation. Naturally, bread will keep better under refrigeration.

Freezing Bread

Bread—every type of bread—freezes very successfully, and will keep several months if well wrapped. Before a loaf is frozen it should be thoroughly cooled, then wrapped tightly in plastic and placed in a plastic bag or wrapped in foil and sealed with binding tape. After it has been labeled and dated, it is ready for the freezer.

To thaw, leave at room temperature or wrap in aluminum foil and heat through—20 to 40 minutes—in a 350° oven. Bread can also be reconstituted in a microwave oven if it is not overheated. (Since the microwave heats food from the inside out, there is a risk of toughening the bread while the outer appearance remains the same.)

Bread Knives

Bread knives are almost as important as a good oven or good baking pans. The wrong knife can tear bread, especially if the bread is fresh or very soft. Fortunately, in the last few years we have had on the market a great variety of good knives with serrated edges, such as the one shown in the drawing. The long-bladed slicing knife intended for meats is also an exceedingly good bread knife, as it will cut through difficult crusts as well as slice thinly. Then there is a kitchen knife with a special type of serrated blade designed just for bread. One of the few attractive features of an electric carving knife is the fact that it cuts huge pumpernickel or rye loaves into paper-thin slices that you cannot get by hand; it is also very good for very crisp crusts. Very sharp slicing knives and French knives will slice bread efficiently too, but they do not have the easy sawing action serrated edges provide. When you are slicing crusty breads (this goes for French bread and sandwich bread), it is much better to slice from the side of the loaf than from the top. It is also easier to guide your knife when slicing from the side.

It goes without saying that your knives should always be very sharp. A serrated knife can be sharpened on a steel—but only the flat side.

Bread and Butter

Good bread and good butter go together. They are one of the perfect marriages in gastronomy, and they never fail to cheer me. I enjoy soft sweet butter spread on paper-thin slices of fresh bread to go with my tea, or on slices of beautiful sweet bread or hot brioche bread. For a special treat I relish the taste of bread and butter with a slice of raw onion, or a hearty, crusty slice of Italian or French bread with butter and a bit of cheese. Also, I find thin brown bread—rye, pumpernickel, or any of the dark breads—and butter wonderfully agreeable with oysters and other such seafood.

Then there are bread and butter sandwiches. The bread can be white, whole wheat, rye, or any kind you like, but it must be sliced very, very thin and spread very thickly with sweet butter. The sandwiches, which should be cool, not warm and runny, can be cut into fingers, diamonds, or triangles. I like them in rather hearty fingers to pack and carry on picnics. They are superb with seafood and delicious with cold chicken, cold turkey, or any cold meat—a much happier choice than rolls. They are also nice to serve with salad, when it is a separate course.

Then, of course, there is the moment when that warm bread comes from the oven and the aroma envelops you; you just have to sit down with a big slab of fresh bread and butter and a glass of wine.

Toast

It seems to me that one seldom finds toast that is really toasted. Usually it is a flabby piece of warmed bread with a slight color to it. My thoughts go back a long way to the days when I first lived in England and one would still use a toasting fork in front of the fire to toast bread, crumpets, and muffins for tea. Never, never, never has toast smelled or tasted as good, save when it has been done over a toast rack on a stove or over coals. Our electric toasters are extremely efficient, but people do not use them correctly. Bread is not toasted when it takes on color; it must have a change of texture as well. So don't be afraid of darker toast, and put it in a rack afterward so that it crisps instead of sogs. Nothing is as revolting as the plate of toast one usually receives in a restaurant or a hotel; this comes buttered and wrapped in a napkin, and while it may have been crisp when it came from the toaster, it has, in the meantime, steamed to a most unpleasant texture. On the other hand, English toast is often kept too long in a rack, so it becomes cold, although crisp. I am not sure which is the greater crime, particularly when a perfect piece of toast made from good bread is one of the most delicious of foods—and one that any fool can make.

And whatever happened to that delectable dish, milk toast? I used to have it for lunch when I was a child, and it was a comfort when I didn't feel too well. Lovely crisp, buttered toast with hot milk poured over it— a delicious meal indeed. And if you wanted to glamorize it you added cream instead of milk, and more little dabs of butter. Sometimes you even added salt and pepper to make it tastier. Try it with toasted Buttermilk White Bread (page 42) or Mrs. Elizabeth Ovenstad's Bread (page 84), using plenty of butter and hot milk or hot cream. Nothing could be simpler or more satisfying.

Stale Bread

Stale bread can be very useful, so it is foolish to waste it. In fact, a sandwich of rather stale bread with thickly sliced onions is delicious. Otherwise, stale bread can be turned into Melba toast, croutons, or bread crumbs. For Melba toast, slice the bread as thin as you can and dry it out in a 250° oven until just barely colored; store in airtight tins or jars. For croutons, cut the bread into dice or crumbs, place on a baking sheet, and proceed as for Melba toast; pack in plastic bags. It is a boon to have both plain and toasted bread crumbs on hand, and they can be kept in tins or jars at the back of the refrigerator. It is simple enough to make them by using a hand grater, but it is even easier to do them in a blender. In the latter case, cut the bread into small dice and blend only a little at a time, which is actually faster than loading the blender jar and waiting for all the dice to sift down.

Choosing the Right Bread

It is strange how few people, in planning a menu, ever consider what bread goes with what dish, yet I think this is as important as choosing any other item on a menu. Here are some of my recommendations (and you'll find my recipes for each type of bread in the index.)

BREAKFAST BREADS

For simple bread and butter with tea or coffee and preserves:

Buttermilk White Bread
William Melville Childs'
   Health Bread
Swedish Limpa

Irish Whole-Wheat Soda Bread
Pumpernickel
Basic White Bread

SWEETENED BREADS, TOASTED, REHEATED, OR AS IS

Monkey Bread
Sally Lunn
Kugelhopf
Egg Twists
Persimmon Bread

Sour-Cream Coffee Cake
Doughnuts
Maple Bars
Filled Doughnuts

Basic White Bread
English Muffin Bread
Challah
Italian Feather Bread
Brioche Bread
Oatmeal Bread

Whole-Meal Bread with
   Potatoes
Any of the Rye Breads
Cinnamon Bread
Raisin and Nut Bread
Portuguese Sweet Bread

TOAST AS A FOUNDATION FOR FINNAN HADDIE, CREAMED CODFISH, SCRAMBLED EGGS, AND OTHER SAVORY DISHES

English Muffin Bread
Basic White Bread
Rye Bread
Pumpernickel

Oatmeal Bread
Griddle Cakes
   Yeast Buckwheat Cakes
   Yeast Pancakes

BREADS FOR LUNCHEON WITH HORS D'OEUVRES, SALADS, COLD MEATS, AND OTHER COLD DISHES

Rolls
Baking Powder Biscuits
Soda Bread
Raw Apple Bread

Thinly sliced Pumpernickel
Rye
Pizza Caccia Nanza
Pita, especially with filling

FILLED BREADS AS A COURSE FOR LUNCH OR LATE SUPPER

Lahma bi Ajeen
Pizza Loaf

Pissaladière

WITH HOT DISHES

Baking Powder Biscuits
Parker House Rolls
Jane Grigson's Walnut Bread
Cornmeal Bread
Anadama Bread

Myrtle Allen's Brown Bread
Sally Lunn
Helen Evans Brown's Corn
   Chili Bread
Bread Sticks

SANDWICH BREADS

For sweet sandwiches

Carl Gohs' Zucchini Bread
Banana Nut Bread

Pistachio Bread

For savory sandwiches
    Brioche Bread
    Finnish Sour Rye Bread
    Bavarian Rye Bread

Whole-Meal Bread with
    Potatoes

BREADS FOR AFTERNOON TEA OR COFFEE

These breads should be cut very thin, buttered with sweet butter, and arranged on a nice serving dish.

White Free-Form Loaf
Sour-Cream Bread
Mrs. Elizabeth Ovenstad's Bread
Maryetta's Oatmeal Bread
Water-Proofed Bread
Italian Holiday Bread
Raisin and Nut Bread
Norwegian Flatbread

Pistachio Bread
Swedish Limpa
Carl Gohs' Zucchini Bread
Persimmon Bread
Gingerbread
Quick Cranberry Bread
Lefse

HOT BREADS

Girdle Scones
Crumpets
Potato Scones

Baking Powder Biscuits (tiny
    ones)

DINNER BREADS

With first courses. With oysters, clams, smoked salmon, smoked sturgeon, and other dishes—thinly sliced and buttered or made into very thin bread-and-butter sandwiches.

Bavarian Rye Bread
Myrtle Allen's Brown Bread
Pumpernickel

Norwegian Whole-Wheat Bread
Verterkake

With soup

Melba Toast made from George
    Lang's Potato Bread,
    Buttermilk White Bread, or
    Cornmeal Bread

Bread Sticks
Thinly sliced and toasted English
    Muffin Bread

Main-course breads
- Alvin Kerr's Zephyr Buns
- Parker House Rolls
- Helen Evans Brown's Corn
  - Chili Bread
- Gingerbread
- Irish Whole-Wheat Soda Bread
- Baking Powder Biscuits
- French-Style Bread
- Saffron Buns

Breads with cheese
- French-Style Bread
- George Lang's Potato Bread
- White Free-Form Loaf
- Cheese Bread
- Pizza Caccia Nanza
- Dark Herb Bread
- Cracked-Wheat Bread

BREADS FOR SPECIAL DIETS
- Gluten Bread
- Salt-Free Water-Proofed Bread

BASIC YEAST BREAD AND OTHER WHITE-FLOUR BREADS

Basic White
Basic Home-Style
White Free-Form Loaf
Broiled White Free-Form Loaf
Buttermilk White
Carl Gohs'
French-Style
Pullman Loaf or Pain de Mie
Refrigerator Potato
George Lang's Potato, with
　Caraway Seeds

Sour-Cream
Jane Grigson's Walnut, from
　Southern Burgundy
Cornmeal
Cheese
Pizza Caccia Nanza
Gluten
Plain Saffron
Italian Feather
Salt-Rising
Sourdough

Basic White Bread

This is my idea of a good, simple loaf of bread—firm, honest in flavor, tender to the bite yet with a slight chewiness in the crust, and excellent for toast. The ingredients are just flour, water, salt, and yeast, with the addition of a little sugar. It is a recipe I use constantly, although I vary it from time to time, and I have chosen it as my first recipe here because I think it will provide any beginner with the basic techniques of breadmaking. In fact, it is one I have taught to my pupils through the years. Once you have mastered the procedures given here, you can go on to more complex recipes without difficulty.

As I have said in the introductory observations, there are many variables in breadmaking. As far as flours are concerned, for example, since I know that the hard wheat flour producing the best results in wheat breads is not always easy to come by, in this recipe we'll use a common unbleached (or bleached) all-purpose flour. And since compressed yeast is often difficult to find and the dry variety is available everywhere, throughout this book we'll use "active dry yeast" and refer to the measure by package, although occasionally I will suggest the alternative of compressed yeast, since many people enjoy working with it. Some breads call for milk or fruit juice; some, like this one, are made with water. The salt content of bread is adjustable too: I use a rule of thumb of 1 tablespoon for each pound (3¾ cups) of flour; you may alter this to your own taste. There are several ways to knead dough, several ways to shape it into a loaf, and it can be given one or more risings. There is also a choice of washes you can use on the loaf before it goes into the oven, and you can slash the top in different styles or leave it as it is. Even the weather has an effect on breadmaking. The degree of humidity and warmth will govern the absorption quality of the flour and the action of the yeast.

Here, in this first recipe, we'll reduce decisions to a minimum and put all of these extra factors into footnotes. You should be able to make this loaf successfully the first time around without referring to a single one of the notes. But they will come in handy as you vary ingredients and develop your own style of baking. For instance, if you have small hands, you will probably prefer to use two hands for kneading. The approach to making every loaf of bread is essentially the same, and for that reason you should implicitly have this recipe in mind throughout the rest of the book, as I will not keep spelling out fundamental procedures, such as how to proof or how to knead.

[1 large loaf or two smaller loaves]

> 1 package active dry yeast
> 1½ to 2 cups warm water (100° to 115°, approximately)
> 2 teaspoons granulated sugar
> 3¾ to 4 cups all-purpose flour (approximately 1 pound)
> 1 tablespoon salt
> 1½ to 2 tablespoons softened butter
>   for buttering bowl and pan

◀? This recipe will make 1 large loaf using the approximate 9 x 5 x 3-inch pan, or 2 smaller loaves, using the approximate 8 x 4 x 2.

First, proof the yeast, which means testing it to make sure it is still active. To do this, pour the contents of the package into ½ cup of the warm water (about 100° to 115°), add the sugar, stir well, and set aside. After a few minutes the fermentation of the yeast will become apparent as the mixture swells and small bubbles appear here and there on the surface.[1]

yeast fermenting

While the yeast is proofing, measure 3¾ cups unsifted flour into a 2- to 3-quart bowl with rounded sides. (Save the other ¼ cup flour for kneading, if necessary.) Add the tablespoon of salt and blend well.[2] Pour approximately ¾ cup warm water[3] into the flour and stir it in with a wooden spoon or with your hands. Add the yeast mixture, and continue stirring until the ingredients are thoroughly blended and tend to form a ball that breaks away from the sides of the bowl. (If the dough is very stiff, add a tiny bit more water.) Transfer the dough to a lightly floured marble slab, bread board, or counter top.

Now begin the kneading process, which evenly distributes the fermenting yeast cells through the dough. There are several ways to knead,[4] but I prefer this one-handed method: Sprinkle the dough lightly with flour and also flour your working hand. Push the heel of your hand down into the dough and away from you. Fold the dough over, give it a quarter turn, and push again with the hand. Continue the sequence of pushing, folding, and turning until it becomes a rhythmic motion. Knead until the dough no longer feels sticky and has a smooth, satiny, elastic texture, adding more flour, if necessary; this will take anywhere from 4 to 10 minutes, de-

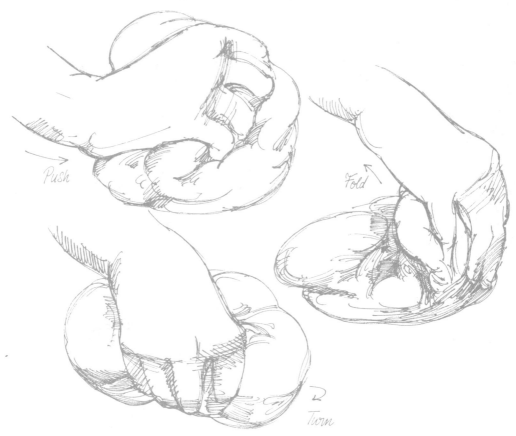

pending on the character of the
flour and the warmth and
humidity of the room. To
test whether the dough has
been kneaded enough, make
an indentation in it with
your fingers; it should
spring back. Sometimes blisters
will form on the surface of
the dough and break, which
is another sign that the kneading is sufficient.

When the dough has reached the consistency described above—with
experience you will know what this means by the feel of it—it is ready for
the first rising. (Rising allows the fermenting yeast to produce tiny bubbles
of carbon dioxide, which stretches the gluten in the flour and thus
leavens the bread.) First, rest the dough on the board for several minutes.
Meanwhile, wash out the mixing bowl, dry it, and rub it with 1 to 1½
tablespoons of softened butter.[5]

Place the ball of dough in the bowl, and roll it around so that it becomes completely coated with butter. (This will keep the surface from drying out and cracking as the dough rises.) Cover the bowl with a piece of
plastic wrap or foil or with a towel and set in a warm, draft-free place.
(The term "draft-free," which you will encounter repeatedly, is used
because the yeast must be pampered with constant warmth to keep it
active.) Find a protected corner or shelf, or use a cool oven (it won't hurt
if the pilot light is on). Allow the dough to double in bulk, which will
take about 1 to 2 hours.

It is difficult for a beginner to tell when dough has actually doubled
in volume, but the increase is dramatically more than one might expect.
You can get the idea best by pouring 4 cups of water into the empty bowl

Basic Yeast Bread and Other White-Flour Breads / 25

(before it has been greased) and then pouring in the same amount again, noting how high up the water comes. Fortunately there is another, surer test to show when the dough is properly risen. When it looks ready, simply make an indentation in it with two fingers. If the dough *does not* spring back, then it is ready. It will not hurt should it rise a little too much, but excessive rising will affect the flavor and texture of the finished bread. If for some reason you must prolong a rising, place the bowl of dough in the refrigerator to slow down the action of the yeast.

after first rising

The dough must now undergo a second rising, which will take place in the baking pan. Thoroughly butter one or two heavily tinned loaf pans.[6] Then remove the cover from the bowl and deflate the dough by pushing down into it with your fist. Transfer it to a floured board, knead it rather well for about 3 minutes, then pat it into a smooth round or oval shape. Let it rest for 4 to 5 minutes, then form it into a loaf about 8 inches long and 3 inches wide.[7] Lift it carefully, drop it into the loaf pan, and smooth it out.

Cover the loaf pan, as you did the bowl, and set it in a warm, draft-free place to double in bulk, at which point the loaf will have risen slight-

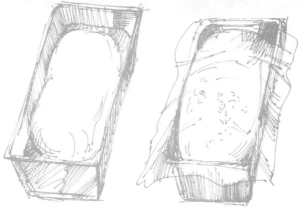

ly above the edge of the pan. The second rising will take anywhere from 40 minutes to 1¼ hours, according to the warmth of the room and the way you have worked the dough. Don't rush the process, and watch the dough carefully. Meanwhile, set the oven for 400°.[8]

There are various ways to treat the loaf before it goes into the oven. For this recipe, merely brush the dough with cold water, which helps to give the top a textured crust.[9] Then, with a sharp knife make three diagonal slashes about ½ inch deep across the top of the loaf, both for a more

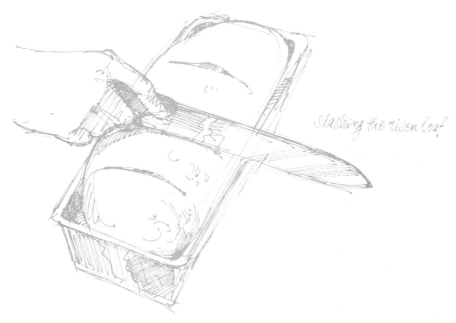

slashing the risen loaf

professional look and to prevent cracking.[10] Place the pan near the center of the lower oven rack and set a timer for 35 minutes. Begin testing after that time, even though the total baking time may be as much as 50 minutes. To test, rap the top of the loaf with your knuckles. When done, it will sound hollow. Invert the loaf onto a towel held in one hand and test the bottom as well for that hollow sound. If it does not seem quite firm enough and needs only a little more baking, place the loaf directly on the oven rack to crisp the bottom, watching it carefully to prevent it from burning. If the test shows that the bottom is somewhat soft, slide the loaf back into the heated pan and return it to the oven to bake for 5 or 6 minutes more. Test the bottom again, and when firm enough, bake the unmolded loaf a few minutes for the final crisping. When completely baked, remove from the oven and set on a bread rack to cool.

After 2 or 3 hours the bread is good for slicing. When it is thoroughly cooled it can be stored in a plastic bag, in or out of the refrigerator, for several days. It also freezes well, and a frozen loaf, wrapped airtight, can be stored for a month. To reheat, remove from the freezer, wrap in aluminum foil, and heat in a 350° oven for about 20 to 40 minutes.

NOTES

1. If you use compressed yeast, crumble it into a measuring cup, add the sugar, and cream the two ingredients together with a spoon for a minute or two, until the mixture becomes quite soft and runny; this helps activate the yeast. Add the warm water—in this instance no warmer than 95°.

2. I feel that 1 tablespoon of salt to 1 pound of flour is the right seasoning, but some people feel it is too much. You can increase or decrease the amount according to your taste. (A sweet bread, for instance, may not take as much.)

3. Milk can be used instead of water; it makes a somewhat richer bread.

4. Here are three alternative ways to knead:

A. Push into the dough with the heel of your right hand (if you are right-handed), then fold the dough toward you, at the same time giving the mass a quarter turn with your left hand, pulling it toward you; this is one continuous circular motion. Repeat the procedure, increasing your speed. It sounds complicated but is in fact quite simple and fast, and it gives a better fold.

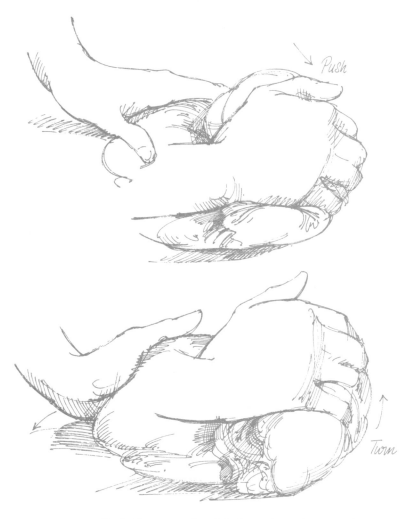

B. Many people prefer to knead with both hands. In this procedure you push into the dough with the heels of the hands, fold the dough over, and give it a quarter turn before pushing again.

C. You can use the dough hook in the electric mixer; see description on page 10.

5. You can also use vegetable oil.

6. You can also use aluminum, aluminum foil, stainless steel, or glass.

7. Here are two alternative ways to shape a loaf:

A. Pat or roll the dough into a strip about as wide as the bottom of the loaf pan and approximately three times the length of the pan. Lightly mark the dough into thirds or just visualize the divisions. Fold the first third over the middle third, and pinch the edges together very well. Fold the final third over the other two thirds, again pinching the edges together. Then with both hands plump the loaf and fit it into the buttered pan.

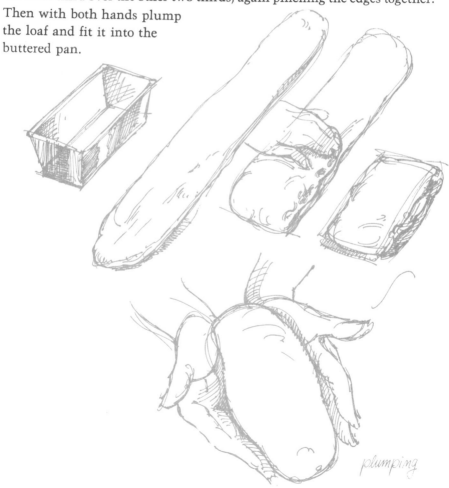

plumping

B. Roll out the dough, and then roll it up into a sausage shape.
Tuck the ends under and fit it, seam side down, in the buttered pan.

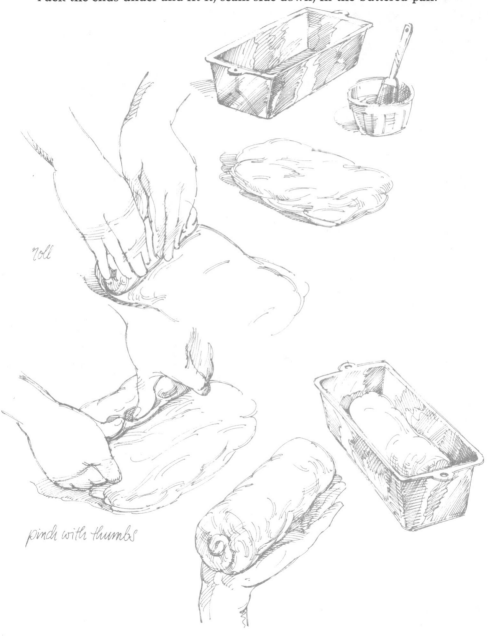

roll

pinch with thumbs

8. When using glass for baking, always set the temperature 25 degrees lower than is specified, since glass heats faster than metal and holds the heat longer.

9. The dough can also be brushed with a mixture of lightly beaten egg whites and water, which colors the crust and makes it very crisp, or it can be brushed with a mixture of beaten egg yolk and milk, cream, or water, which gives the crust a rich brown color.

10. The loaf can also be slashed lengthwise down the center.

VARIATION

• **Whole-Wheat Bread:** This same recipe can be used to make a whole-wheat loaf. Merely use 2 cups whole-wheat flour and 1¾ to 2 cups white flour. For a slightly richer loaf, add 3 to 4 tablespoons olive oil or peanut' oil to the flour before adding the water, and use slightly less water to compensate for the oil.

REMEDIES FOR THE NOT-QUITE-PERFECT SLICE

• *If your slice sags more than the one on the next page and is soggy to the bite, the dough was not aerated enough. It probably had too much liquid and did not get enough kneading. Next time work in a bit more flour as you knead and keep at it longer.*

• *If your dough seems to have a pretty good crumb but tastes damp, it means that it did not bake long enough. Try putting it in the oven at a slightly lower temperature at the start and let it cook longer.*

• *If your loaf has really fallen flat and doughy, gooey streaks appear in the slices, the chances are that the second rising was too long and the bread collapsed on contact with the heat. Be careful not to let the loaves rise too much in the pans.*

• *If your bread has risen more on one side than on the other, you probably had it in the wrong position in the oven. And if the slice has an uneven crumb, this is certainly true. Next time be sure to place a single*

The Perfect Slice

loaf in the center of the oven so that uneven distribution of heat won't upset the form and shape of the loaf while it is baking. Usually, if you have several loaves in the oven, evenly spaced, this problem will not occur, since the flow of air around the pans will be regular.

• If your loaf has cracked on one side during the baking, don't worry. It is likely to be a perfectly good loaf—in fact, it may be utterly delicious— even if it doesn't look beautiful. This is something that at times even the best bakers can't prevent.

• If the bottom and side crusts are pale and soft and the bread is difficult to slice without having to saw with a very sharp knife, next time remove the bread from the pan and place it on the rack or on tiles in the warm oven to brown and crisp the bottom and sides, turning the loaves once, before cooling. (Also, do not ever wrap loaves in plastic before they are thoroughly cooled.)

• If your bread has really mushroomed and there is a rather deep indentation around the bottom, it means that the entire loaf has broken away from the bottom crust, probably because you tried to pack too much dough into too small a pan, or, if you were making a free-form loaf, your oven was undoubtedly too hot at first so that the bottom cooked too quickly and as the loaf rose it broke away and mushroomed. In either case you'll have an uneven slice, denser at the bottom than at the top, but this is no great tragedy.

• If your free-form loaf spread too much as it was rising, your dough was too soft. Free-form loaves must be quite firm when shaped. Next time remember to add extra flour as you are kneading and if you are still uncertain put the dough in a ring to contain it.

• If, when slicing your bread, you find that the top crust separates from the rest, it means your loaf was not properly formed and the heat caused instant aeration when it was put in the oven. This is not a serious matter and sometimes happens even with commercial breads. To remedy, try one of the alternate methods of forming to get a tighter loaf.

• Large holes in your bread indicate that you may have overkneaded or that the dough rose too long. This is an advantage with certain free-form loaves, particularly French, but with other breads an even crumb is one of the attributes of good baking. All this is really a matter of taste, however, and if you really like a strong bread with big holes and a chewy texture, given the dough lots of kneading and a long, slow rise—even two risings.

• If there are circular streaks in your slice, don't worry. They are usually caused by the rolling and pinching of the dough when you formed your loaf, and you probably pinched too vigorously.

• If your slice has doughy or small, hard lumps, it is certain that the original dough was not mixed sufficiently, possibly because it got too stiff to handle. Next time hold back on the flour so that the dough gets thoroughly mixed, then work in additional flour as you knead.

Basic Home-Style Bread

To most people homemade bread means a slightly sweet loaf made with milk and some shortening, quite light and rather fine in texture and much enjoyed when fresh with a generous spreading of butter and preserves. It is also popular for sandwiches and toast. Here is such a loaf, which I call "home-style" to distinguish it from my other basic white bread.

[2 loaves]

> 1 package active dry yeast
> 2 cups warm milk (100° to 115°, approximately)
> 2 tablespoons granulated sugar
> 1/4 cup melted butter
> 1 tablespoon salt
> 5 to 6 cups all-purpose flour
> 1 egg white, lightly beaten (optional)

⊷Add the yeast to ½ cup of the warm milk, along with the 2 tablespoons sugar, and stir well until the yeast is completely dissolved. Allow the yeast to proof. Place the remaining milk, the melted butter, and the salt in a bowl. Stir in the flour, 1 cup at a time, with a wooden spoon. After the third cup, add the yeast mixture. Continue stirring in flour until the mixture is rather firm, which should take about 4 to 5 cups. Remove the dough to a floured board or a marble slab, and knead, adding more flour as necessary if it gets sticky, until it is supple, satiny, and no longer sticky. Butter a bowl and place the dough in it, turning to coat all sides with the fat. Cover and allow to rise in a warm, draft-free spot until doubled in bulk, about 1½ to 2 hours.

Deflate the dough by punching it firmly two or three times, return to the floured board, and knead 4 to 5 minutes more. Divide into two equal parts and shape into loaves. Place in well-buttered 9 x 5 x 3-inch loaf tins, cover, and let rise again until doubled in bulk. Slash the loaves with a sharp knife and brush with lightly beaten egg white or water. Bake in a 400° oven for 40 to 45 minutes or until the bread sounds hollow when tapped with the knuckles. Remove the loaves from the pans and put them in oven a few minutes longer to become crisped.

White Free-Form Loaf

A free-form loaf is one that is not baked in a tin. It can be made round or oval. It is best, I find, when baked in an oven in which the racks are lined with tiles (see page 12), with a pan of boiling water set on the lower rack to create steam. This type of bread is known as a "sponge loaf," which means that you make a soft yeast mixture and let it refrigerate one or two nights to start fermentation before you continue with the recipe.

[1 free-form loaf]

FOR THE SPONGE:
2 packages active dry yeast
½ cup warm water (100° to 115°, approximately)
2 cups flour, preferably hard wheat
¾ to 1 cup water, approximately

◄ᕤ Dissolve the yeast in the warm water, let it proof in a large mixing bowl, and start adding the flour with enough water to make quite a soft dough. When the sponge is well mixed, cover it with a plate or plastic wrap and refrigerate it 12 to 36 hours—one or two nights.

FOR THE BREAD:
3 tablespoons olive or other vegetable oil
½ cup buttermilk
2 cups flour plus ½ cup for kneading
1 tablespoon coarse salt
Cornmeal

◄ᕤ When ready to make the bread, remove the sponge from the refrigerator, punch down, and place in a large mixing bowl. Add the oil, then gradually add the buttermilk and 2 cups of flour, mixed with the salt, to make a soft dough. Turn this out onto a lightly floured board, using another ½ cup flour or more, if need be, and knead for a good 10 minutes, until the dough is smooth, elastic, and resilient to the pressure of your

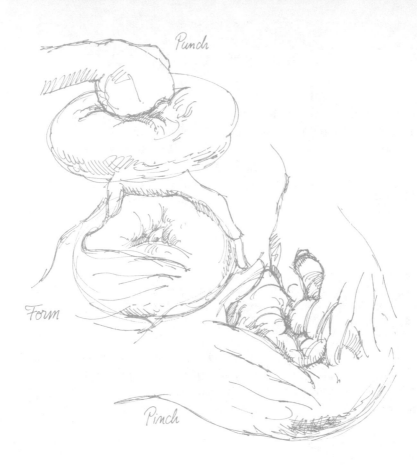

Punch

Form

Pinch

fingers. Shape into a ball, and place in a buttered or oiled bowl, turning to lightly coat with the fat. Let rise until doubled in bulk at ordinary room temperature. (Because the sponge is cold when it comes from the refrigerator, rising will probably take from 1½ to 2 hours, or even a little more.) When it has risen, punch down and let rest for a few minutes, then remove to a floured board and knead for 3 to 4 minutes. Place back in the bowl and let rise a second time until doubled in bulk, 1 to 1¼ hours.

Punch the dough down again and let rest for 2 or 3 minutes on the floured board, then shape into an oval, round, or oblong loaf and place on an ungreased sheet coated with cornmeal. Let rise in a warm, draft-free place until doubled in size, 1 to 2 hours—don't worry if it's slow. (If the dough seems to have spread a lot, resist the temptation to reshape it; it will make a good loaf anyway.) Preheat the oven to 425°, and set a pan of boiling water on the lower rack. Brush the loaf with cold water and slash about ½ inch deep in several places with a razor blade or a very sharp knife. Let rest at room temperature for about 5 more minutes, then place the baking sheet in the oven, on the upper rack. Immediately lower the temperature to 375°, bake for 20 minutes, then brush again with cold water. Continue to bake for 40 to 50 minutes longer, until the bread is a delicious-looking dark color and makes a hollow sound when tapped on top and bottom. Cool thoroughly before slicing.

Broiled White Free-Form Loaf

This was a mistake that proved to be extremely interesting. I was testing another version of the free-form loaf, the recipe for which appears below, turned the oven to 375° without my glasses on, and placed the loaf in the oven. I thought it was browning magnificently and then discovered I had turned the oven to "broil." I immediately switched to "bake," but by this time I had a beautifully brown, crisp top crust and the loaf had risen. In the end the loaf tasted absolutely wonderful, and the upper crust was superb. The next time I reversed the procedure and let it bake first and then broil, and this loaf came out very well too. I thought I would record my experience here as a novelty—and to make the point that baking bread is always an adventure.

[1 free-form loaf]

2 packages active dry yeast
¾ cup warm water (100° to 115°, approximately)
4 cups unbleached all-purpose flour
1½ tablespoons coarse salt
3 tablespoons olive, vegetable, or peanut oil
½ cup buttermilk
Cornmeal
1 egg white, beaten with 1 tablespoon water

•ℰDissolve the yeast in the warm water and let it proof. Measure the flour into a mixing bowl, add the salt, and blend well. Add the yeast and blend thoroughly, preferably with your hands. Add the oil, and then, gradually, the buttermilk. Mix with the hands or in an electric mixer with a dough hook until the dough comes off the bowl. Turn out onto a lightly floured board and knead for 10 minutes, until the dough is smooth and resilient. Remove to a buttered bowl and turn to coat the surface with butter. Cover and let rise until doubled in bulk.

Punch the dough down, knead for 3 minutes, and let rise once more. Punch down again, then, using both hands, gather the dough into a big circular package, draw the top together to close it, and pinch the ends together. Turn the dough over, and set it, pinched-end side down, on a baking sheet sprinkled with cornmeal, and let rise until doubled in bulk. (Cornmeal may be sprinkled on the top, too, for an extra accent.) Slash the top in three places and brush with the egg wash. Broil at 375° for 20 minutes, then switch to "bake" for 25 minutes, or until the loaf sounds hollow when tapped with the knuckles. (If your broiler has no setting, place the bread as far as possible from the unit and watch carefully. You may have to switch from "broil" to "bake" more quickly.) Remove the loaf from the baking sheet and let it rest directly on the oven rack for a few minutes to brown the bottom. Cool on a rack.

The Perfect Free-Form Loaf
(see pages 33–35 for talk on imperfections and remedies)

Buttermilk White Bread

Made with hard-wheat flour, this loaf is light, chewy, and extremely well crusted. It is a delicious bread for sandwiches or for toast, and it stores nicely if refrigerated in a plastic bag or frozen. The dough can also be baked as small rolls (see pages 188–9 for forming).

[1 loaf]

2 packages active dry yeast
1 tablespoon granulated sugar
½ cup warm water (100° to 115°, approximately)
4 cups unbleached hard-wheat flour
1 tablespoon salt
3 tablespoons melted butter
1 to 1½ cups buttermilk

❧Combine the yeast, sugar, and water and allow to proof. Mix the flour, salt, melted butter, and buttermilk together, work into a smooth dough, and then add the yeast mixture. Beat well for 2 minutes, then remove to a well-floured board and knead for approximately 10 minutes, until the dough is supple, smooth, and satiny. (The dough can also be prepared in an electric mixer equipped with a dough hook. Combine all the ingredients, knead with the dough hook for approximately 5 to 6 minutes, and then remove the dough to a floured board for about 2 minutes of kneading by hand.) Place the dough in a buttered bowl and turn to coat the dough with butter. Cover and set in a warm spot to rise until more than doubled in bulk. Punch down the dough, remove to a floured board, and knead for two minutes. Form into a loaf about 9 x 5 inches by patting flat to a rather rough rectangle, folding in the ends, and then folding in the sides. Pinch the seams together well. Put in a buttered 9 x 5 x 3-inch bread pan, cover, and place in a warm, draft-free spot to rise until more than doubled in bulk. Bake in the center of a preheated 375° oven for about 40 minutes. For rolls, bake at 375° for 18 to 20 minutes. Remove from the pan, and bake for another 5 to 8 minutes on its side to give a crisp brown crust. Cool on a rack before slicing.

Carl Gohs' Bread

Carl Gohs is a fellow Oregonian who has done much research on early foods, as well as on pioneer and Indian cooking. His bread is quite a lot of trouble to make, but it has interesting flavor, because of the wheat germ, and the texture is also extremely good. The intriguing thing about this recipe is that the final dough is twisted to make it denser, which results in a fine grain. It is a beautiful bread that keeps well, whether stored in a plastic bag in the refrigerator or frozen, and it ships nicely too. (It was flown from coast to coast when I first tasted it.) It's fun to make a big batch and save some, or give it to friends.

[2 loaves]

3 packages active dry yeast
½ cup warm water (100° to 115°, approximately)
1 tablespoon brown sugar
5 cups unbleached all-purpose flour
1 medium potato, unpeeled but washed
1½ cups potato water
1 cup wheat germ
½ cup powdered milk
5 teaspoons salt
Butter, at room temperature

◄ In a 2-quart or medium-large mixing bowl, dissolve yeast in the ½ cup lukewarm water, add the brown sugar, stir, and set aside for 15 to 20 minutes, until it works and froths, acquiring about a 2-inch "head." Stir in ½ cup flour and continue to stir until smooth. Set this "sponge" aside to work, covered with a cloth, for about an hour. Stir it down each time it doubles in bulk.

Meanwhile, cut the washed, unpeeled potato in several pieces and boil in about 1½ cups water until tender. Peel and mash. Measure the water remaining in pan and add to it, if necessary, to bring it to 1½ cups. Combine the mashed potatoes and potato water, stir, and set aside to cool.

In a bowl of at least 6-quart capacity or, better yet, in a stainless steel pan with straight sides and flat bottom, combine 2½ cups of flour (including any of the flours listed under "variations" below) with wheat germ, powdered milk, and salt. Stir well with a fork. When the yeast mixture has doubled in bulk and been deflated at least two times, add it to the dry ingredients in the large bowl along with the potato slurry. Stir 1 or 2 minutes with wooden spoon, until all the ingredients are blended. Cover with a cloth and set this second sponge aside in a warm, draft-free place to double in bulk, about 1½ to 1¾ hours.

Take 1 cup of flour and spread it into a 14-inch circle on a board at least 16 by 18 inches. Spoon out the bread dough onto the flour, then wash the bowl or pan the dough was in, and butter it liberally. Set bowl aside.

Take the last cup of flour, sprinkle some of it over the dough on the board, and begin to knead the dough, scooping it up from below and turning it over frequently to incorporate the flour. Add the remaining flour and knead vigorously until the dough is smooth and elastic. (The total kneading time will be 10 to 12 minutes.) Roll the ball of dough in the well-buttered bowl or pan to coat evenly. Cover with a cloth and set aside in a warm, draft-free place to double in bulk, about 1 to 1½ hours. Butter hands lightly, punch the dough down, divide in half, and form into 2 loaves. Place each in a buttered 9 x 5 x 3-inch baking pan. Cover with cloths and set aside in a warm, draft-free place to double in bulk, about 1 hour to 1 hour 10 minutes.

Arrange the pans on a single rack in the center of a preheated 450° oven. Reduce the heat immediately to 400° and bake for 40 minutes, or until the loaves are dark brown and rapping on top produces a hollow sound.

Turn the loaves out onto a wire rack to cool.

VARIATIONS

• Substitute for 1 cup of white flour any of the following: 1 cup stone-ground flour, 1 cup rye flour, 1 cup whole-wheat flour, or ½ cup rye and ½ cup whole-wheat.

NOTE

Mr. Gohs twists the dough after it has been formed into a loaf, stretching it between his two hands and turning it clockwise several times at one end while turning counterclockwise at the other, in the way in which you would gently wring out a towel. He then fits it into the pan. You will find that this gives an interesting and unusual texture to the bread.

Stretching and twisting

French-Style Bread

French bread, as we all know, has been praised and prized above all other breads in the world for its distinctive crumb, crisp crust, and superb flavor. However, the carefully controlled preparation of it in commercial bakeries is difficult to duplicate in one's own kitchen. If you are ready for the challenge, you should search out a recipe that is as complete as the one developed by Julia Child and Simone Beck for Volume 2 of *Mastering the Art of French Cooking.* Their method seems tremendously complex but it is great fun to follow through to the final goal (and once mastered, not difficult to do again); the loaves are startlingly good and genuinely French.

The bread I am giving here is not truly French, and for that reason it is called "French-style." Actually it could be called "Continental," because it is very much like the bread one finds in Italy, Spain, and Portugal. It has also been known for many years as "Cuban bread." It is a casual, easy-to-make bread that can be played with in several ways. If made according to the basic recipe below it produces a good loaf ready for eating almost the minute it comes from the oven. It will not hold for more than half a day but, of course, can be frozen (see page 13).

[2 long loaves]

1½ packages active dry yeast
1 tablespoon granulated sugar
2 cups warm water (100° to 115°, approximately)
1 tablespoon salt
5 to 6 cups all-purpose or hard-wheat flour
3 tablespoons yellow cornmeal
1 tablespoon egg white, mixed with 1 tablespoon cold water

◄ Combine the yeast with sugar and warm water in a large bowl and allow to proof. Mix the salt with the flour and add to the yeast mixture, a cup at a time, until you have a stiff dough. Remove to a lightly floured board and knead until no longer sticky, about 10 minutes, adding flour as necessary. Place in a buttered bowl and turn to coat the surface with butter. Cover and let rise in a warm place until doubled in bulk, 1½ to 2 hours.

Punch down the dough. Turn out on a floured board and shape into two long, French bread-style loaves. Place on a baking sheet that has been sprinkled with the cornmeal but not buttered. Slash the tops of the loaves diagonally in two or three places, and brush with the egg wash. Place in a cold oven, set the temperature at 400°, and bake 35 minutes, or until well browned and hollow sounding when the tops are rapped.

VARIATIONS

• For a wheaten loaf, use half white flour and half whole-wheat flour.

• Substitute equal parts of whole-wheat flour and cracked wheat for half of the white flour.

• For a more involved, more tightly textured loaf: Use either the original recipe or the whole-wheat variation. After the first rising, remove from the bowl, punch down, and knead again for 5 to 10 minutes. Return to the buttered bowl for a second rising. When it has doubled in bulk, form into two loaves and place on a baking sheet sprinkled with cornmeal. Cover and let rise for 30 minutes. Slash with a sharp razor or knife, brush with slightly beaten egg white or water, and place in a cold oven set for 375° or 400°. Bake until nicely browned and hollow sounding when tapped with the knuckles.

• Line the oven rack with tiles (see page 12), preheat the oven to 400°, and slide your bread loaves from the baking sheet directly onto the tiles, which have been sprinkled with cornmeal.

• Add to the liquid in the first step 4 to 5 tablespoons olive oil and then proceed with either the original recipe or the whole-wheat variation. You may need to use a small additional amount of flour.

• Use ⅓ white flour, ⅓ whole-wheat, and ⅓ cracked-wheat. This will give a very nice coarse, nutlike texture to the bread. With this mixture I would advise adding olive oil in the beginning to give tenderness.

Pullman Loaf or Pain de Mie

This is the white bread frequently used for sandwiches, a four-square loaf that has delicate texture, a fine crumb, and good flavor. It is made in a special pan with a sliding lid at the top that keeps the bread in shape as it bakes. If you do not have this type of pan, you can bake it in an ordinary pan, covered with tinfoil and lightly weighted with tiles or similar weights. However, the tins are easily available in restaurant and baking supply houses and are not expensive. This is a beautiful toasting bread, and if correctly made, it can be sliced paper thin. In addition to its excellence for sandwiches and toast, it is useful for croutons, crumbs, rolled sandwiches, little canapés, and hors d'oeuvres.

[1 large loaf]

> 2 packages active dry yeast
> 1½ cups warm water (100° to 115°, approximately)
> 2 teaspoons granulated sugar
> 6½ cups all-purpose flour
> 1 tablespoon plus 2 teaspoons coarse salt
> 1 stick (½ cup) sweet butter

◄ Dissolve the yeast in ½ cup of the warm water with the sugar, and let it proof. Combine 6 cups of the flour with the salt in a large bowl. Using two knives, cut the butter into the flour and salt, being careful not to overwork it. (Or using your hands, squeeze pieces of the butter into the flour very carefully.) Place the yeast mixture in a large mixing bowl and add ¼ cup warm water. Then add the flour-and-butter mixture, incorporating it with one hand only and using the remaining water to create a stiff, sticky dough. Turn the dough out on a floured board and work it hard for a good 10 minutes: slap it, beat it, punch it, and give it a thorough kneading. When finally smooth, let rest for a few minutes, then shape into a ball. Place in a well-buttered bowl, turn to coat the surface, cover, and let rise in a warm, draft-free spot for 1½ hours.

Punch the dough down and let rise for 3 to 4 minutes, then knead again vigorously for 3 or 4 minutes. Shape into a ball and put back in the buttered bowl to rise again, from 45 minutes to 1 hour. Punch the dough down and let rest another 3 or 4 minutes. Knead a third time and then shape carefully into a loaf to fit a well-buttered 13½ x 4 x 3¾-inch pan.

Let rise until almost doubled in bulk, approximately 1 hour. Butter the inside of the lid, if you are using a pullman tin, or butter a piece of foil, cover (weight if using foil), and place in a preheated 400° oven. Turn the heat down immediately to 375°. After 30 minutes turn the tin on one side for 5 minutes and then on the other side for 5 minutes. Set it upright again, and remove the lid; the bread should have risen to the top of the pan. (If using foil and weights, remove both at this point.)

Continue to bake until it is a golden brown, which will take about 12 to 15 minutes more. Turn the loaf out of the pan and put it directly on the rack of the oven to bake for a few minutes longer, until the bread is a beautiful color and sounds hollow when tapped with the knuckles. Let it cool thoroughly on a rack before slicing.

NOTE

The loaf can be frozen successfully for 2 months, and it will keep well in the refrigerator for several days.

Refrigerator Potato Bread

The potato and butter in this loaf give it a distinctive, very pleasant flavor. Moist and rather heavy in texture, it keeps extremely well in the refrigerator if stored in a plastic bag. It is nice for sandwiches or toast or as a breakfast or tea bread, and is reminiscent of breads that used to be common in the nineteenth century.

[1 round loaf or 2 regular loaves]

1 package active dry yeast
½ cup plus 1 tablespoon granulated sugar
½ cup warm water (100° to 115°, approximately)
1 cup warm milk or potato water (i.e., water
    in which the potatoes were cooked)
1½ sticks (¾ cup) butter, softened
    in the milk or potato water
1½ tablespoons salt
2 eggs
1 cup mashed potatoes (instant mashed
    potatoes can be used)
6 cups all-purpose flour, approximately

◄⅔Dissolve the yeast and tablespoon of sugar in the warm water and let proof for about 5 minutes. Then add the warm milk or potato water, butter, ½ cup sugar, salt, and the eggs to the yeast mixture, and stir to blend thoroughly. Add the mashed potatoes and stir well. Then add the flour, 1 cup at a time, beating well after each addition, to make a thoroughly stiff dough. (You may not need the full 6 cups.) Turn out the dough on a floured board and knead for 10 or 12 minutes, until the dough is very smooth and shows great elasticity. Shape into a ball. Butter a large mixing bowl, place the dough in the bowl, and turn to coat all sides with the butter. Cover tightly and refrigerate overnight to let rise. (In testing, we have refrigerated it as much as 16 to 18 hours.)

Remove from the refrigerator, punch down, and turn out on a floured board. Let rest for 5 to 6 minutes, then knead vigorously for 4 or 5 minutes and let rest again. Shape into two loaves, using either of the methods given on pages 31–2. Place in two well-buttered 9 x 5 x 3-inch tins, or form into a ball and place it in a well-buttered 9-inch pie tin to make a single round loaf. In either case, let the dough rise until it is doubled in bulk. (Because it has been refrigerated for a lengthy period, the rising time may be as long as 4 hours. So be patient.) Preheat the oven to 375° and bake the loaf or loaves for 40 to 45 minutes. Remove the bread from the tins and rap the top and bottom with your knuckles. If you get a hollow sound, it is done. Return the bread, standing free now, to the oven, placing it directly on the oven rack to bake and crisp and color the crust. Cool thoroughly before slicing.

VARIATIONS

• Before baking, brush the loaves with white of egg, lightly beaten, and slash the tops diagonally in two or three places with a very sharp knife or razor blade.

• If you are baking a round loaf, slash the top twice to make a cross, which gives the loaf a nicely finished look.

• Use half whole-meal, whole-wheat, or graham flour.

• If you wish, you may omit the ½ cup sugar entirely.

George Lang's Potato Bread
with Caraway Seeds

This fine example of gutsy Middle European peasant bread, from *The Cuisine of Hungary*, is baked free form, rises well, looks appetizing, and has a delicious "nose." Its pungent flavor is completely different from that of most other breads, and is much better the second day. It also stores well in the refrigerator, and because of its rather tight texture, makes extraordinarily good toast. All in all, it is a most satisfactory loaf of bread, delicious with heavily sauced dishes because it is a perfect dunking bread. It's also great for a bread, cheese, and wine meal.

[1 large free-form loaf]

> 3 medium potatoes, or enough for
>   1 cup mashed potatoes
> 1 package active dry yeast
> 2½ cups warm water (100° to 115°, approximately)
> 2 pounds unbleached all-purpose flour
>   (approximately 8 cups)
> 1½ tablespoons salt
> ½ tablespoon caraway seeds
> Cornmeal (optional)

❧ Scrub the potatoes and boil them in their skins until tender. Drain them, then peel and mash or put through a potato ricer while they are still warm. Allow the potatoes to cool. Dissolve the yeast in ½ cup of the warm water, mix well with 3 tablespoons of the flour in a large bowl, and let this "starter" rise for 30 minutes. Add the remaining 2 cups of warm water, the salt, and the caraway seeds, then add the remainder of the flour and the mashed potatoes and mix well. Turn out on a floured board and knead until the dough is elastic and supple and has great life in it, about 12 to 15 minutes. Shape into a ball. Oil a bowl, put the dough in it, and turn the dough to coat with oil. Place in a warm, draft-free spot for 1 to 2 hours to rise until doubled in bulk.

Remove the dough, punch down, and knead for 4 or 5 minutes. Shape into a large round loaf, place in a buttered 12-inch ovenproof skillet with rounded sides, and let rise for about 30 to 35 minutes. Brush the loaf with water, and then make a deep incision in the form of a cross in the center. Bake it in a preheated 400° oven for 1 hour, or until it is nicely browned and sounds hollow when tapped with the knuckles. (The baking time can vary, taking even as long as 1¼ hours.)

NOTES

1. If you find the dough is not too soft, you might try letting it rise in a free-form shape on a cookie sheet sprinkled with cornmeal. Then slide it directly onto hot tiles to bake (see page 12).

2. You may want more salt in this bread the second time you make it; I find that 2 tablespoons is not too much.

Sour-Cream Bread

This is a very rich bread with a slightly acid flavor and a wonderful texture. I invented it one day when I set out to make buttermilk bread and didn't have any buttermilk. I resorted to sour cream instead, and the results were highly satisfactory. I like it as a fresh bread, with plenty of butter, or as toast, and I must say it also makes delicious sandwiches.

[2 loaves]

1 package active dry yeast
3 tablespoons granulated sugar
¼ cup warm water (100° to 115°, approximately)
2 cups sour cream, at room temperature
1 tablespoon salt
¼ teaspoon baking soda
4½ to 5 cups all-purpose flour

◄ Combine the yeast, sugar, and water, and allow to proof for 5 minutes. Put the sour cream, salt, and soda in a mixing bowl. Add the yeast mixture. Then add 4 cups of the flour, cup by cup, to make a very wet, sticky dough, beating hard with a wooden spoon after each addition. Scrape out onto a lightly floured board. Using a baker's scraper or a spackling knife, lift the flour and the dough, and fold the dough over. Turn it clockwise slightly and repeat the lifting and folding process until the dough is less sticky and can be worked with your hands. Add only enough flour to prevent sticking. (This entire kneading should take about 10 minutes, possibly longer if you are inexperienced.) Shape the dough into a ball, place in a buttered bowl, and turn to coat it with the butter. Cover with plastic and let sit in a warm spot to double in bulk.

Punch the dough down. Turn onto a lightly floured board and knead for a minute, then divide into two equal pieces. Butter two 9 x 5 x 3-inch loaf tins. Shape the dough into loaves and fit into the tins. Cover loosely and let rise again until doubled. Bake in a preheated 375° oven for 30 to 35 minutes, or until the loaves sound hollow when tapped on top and bottom. Cool thoroughly before slicing.

Jane Grigson's Walnut Bread from Southern Burgundy

This recipe comes from a delightful cookbook called *Good Things* by an English writer, Jane Grigson, who has a fine palate and the ability to evoke vivid pictures of food. It makes one of the most attractively flavored and textured breads I have eaten in a long time. If you can't find walnut oil, you can use a fruity olive oil. Baked in intriguing small, round loaves, it is light and has a pleasant crust, delicious "nose," and a delicate onion flavor. It's good with broiled or roasted meats, or with some cheeses, notably goat.

[4 free-form loaves]

5 cups all-purpose flour (preferably unbleached)
1 tablespoon salt
2 tablespoons sugar
2 packages active dry yeast
2 cups warm milk
½ cup walnut oil or 8 tablespoons
    (1 stick) butter, melted but cool
½ cup walnuts, roughly chopped
¾ cup onion, finely chopped

"Sift flour, salt, and sugar into a warm bowl. Dissolve the yeast in ½ cup of warm milk, and pour it into the middle of the flour, together with the walnut oil (or butter) and the rest of the milk. Knead well until the dough is firm and blended into a smooth, springy ball (about 10 minutes). Leave in a warm place to rise for 2 hours (or in a cool place overnight). Punch down the dough, mix in the walnuts and onion, shape into four rounds, and leave on a greased baking tray to rise for 45 minutes. Bake at 400° for 45 minutes, or until the loaves sound hollow when tapped underneath."

Cornmeal Bread

This is a deliciously crunchy loaf with a texture quite different from that of most other breads, although it is somewhat similar to oatmeal bread. I find it best freshly sliced and toasted, and make it often to use for breakfast, since it is a good keeper. It makes a beautiful, well-risen loaf that should be thoroughly cooled before slicing. Don't let the smell of it tempt you into cutting a big chunk off while it is still hot.

[2 loaves]

½ cup cornmeal
1 cup boiling water
1 teaspoon salt
2 packages active dry yeast
½ cup warm water (100° to 115°, approximately)
1 tablespoon granulated sugar
1 cup warm milk
2-3 teaspoons salt
¼ cup dark brown sugar
4 to 4½ cups all-purpose flour (preferably unbleached)

◆ ¿Pour the cornmeal into the boiling water with the salt and stir vigorously until it cooks thick (about 4 minutes). Place it in a large mixing bowl to cool. Proof the yeast with the granulated sugar in the water, then pour into the mixing bowl with the cooled cornmeal mixture. Mix well. Add the warm milk, salt, brown sugar, and flour, 1 cup at a time, stirring very well after each addition of flour. When the mixture is well blended and begins to pull away from the sides of the bowl, turn out on a lightly floured board and knead until smooth and elastic, about 10 to 12 minutes, adding more flour as needed. Butter a large bowl. Place the dough in the bowl and turn to coat with the butter on all sides. Cover and set in a warm, draft-free place to double in bulk.

Punch the dough down and turn out on a lightly floured board. Cut in half, shape into two loaves, and let rest while you butter two 9 x 5 x 3-inch tins. Place the dough in the tins, cover, and let rise again until almost doubled in bulk, or just level with the tops of the baking tins. Bake in a preheated 425° oven for 10 minutes, then lower the temperature to 350° and continue baking for 20 to 25 minutes, until the bread is nicely browned and sounds hollow when removed from the tins and rapped with the knuckles on top and bottom. Place the loaves, without tins, on the oven rack for a few minutes, to crisp the crust. Cool on racks before slicing.

Cheese Bread

This rather unusual bread is delicate and moist, with an intriguing cheese bouquet and flavor. It is ideal for sandwiches, it toasts extremely well, and it makes excellent crumbs when a cheese-flavored topping for certain dishes is called for. You may, of course, combine the crumbs with a little additional grated Parmesan cheese.

[2 loaves]

1 package active dry yeast
  or one ½-ounce cake compressed yeast
1 tablespoon granulated sugar
1¾ cups warm water (100° to 115°, approximately)
5 to 6 cups all-purpose flour
1 tablespoon salt, or slightly more to taste
½ stick (¼ cup) softened butter
1 teaspoon Tabasco
¼ cup freshly grated Parmesan cheese, or slightly more to taste
¾ cup shredded Gruyère or Swiss Emmenthaler cheese

◄ Dissolve the yeast with the sugar in ¼ cup of the warm water and allow to proof. In a large bowl, mix 5 cups of flour and the salt. Make a well in the center and add the remaining 1½ cups warm water, the butter, the Tabasco, and the yeast mixture. Stir with a wooden spoon or spatula or with your floured hands until the dough is well amalgamated. Turn out on a heavily floured board (use about ½ cup flour) and knead for 10 to 12 minutes or until the dough is smooth, elastic, and rather satiny in texture and all the flour on the board is absorbed; add flour if you need it. Place the dough in a buttered or oiled bowl and turn to coat on all sides. Cover with a towel and let rise in a warm, draft-free spot until doubled in bulk, 1½ to 2 hours or slightly more.

Punch down the dough, turn it out on a lightly floured board, and knead in the cheeses. When thoroughly blended, cut the dough in half and let rest for 10 minutes, then roll out each half into a rectangle about 11 x 6 inches and let rest for 2 or 3 minutes more. Roll each rectangle up, pinching the edges as you do so, and tucking in the ends so that the loaf measures about 4½ x 7½ inches (see page 32). Place the dough in two well-buttered 8 x 4 x 2-inch tins, cover, and let rise in a warm spot until the bread has reached the top of the tin or slightly higher, or has more or less doubled in size.

Bake on the center of the middle rack in a preheated 375° oven for approximately 30 minutes, or until the loaves sound hollow when removed from the tins and rapped with the knuckles on both top and bottom. Bake directly on the oven rack, without the tins, for a few minutes to firm the crust. Cool the bread on racks before slicing.

VARIATIONS
• Instead of the butter, use ⅓ cup peanut oil or olive oil. Also use oil for the baking tins.
• Use fresh Parmesan or Romano only—a little over a cup—or use a mixture of the two.
• Use shredded sharp Cheddar instead of the Gruyère cheese.
• Bake as one loaf in a 10 x 4½ x 3-inch pan, which will make a thicker, more concentrated loaf and will take slightly longer to bake.

Pizza Caccia Nanza

This is a recipe of Edward Giobbi's, from his delightful book, *Italian Family Cooking.* "The literal translation of *caccia nanza*," says Mr. Giobbi, "is 'take out before.' When bread was made in traditional Italian households a bit of dough was reserved to make a pizza. The pizza was placed in the oven with the bread and obviously cooked more quickly. It was 'taken out before' the bread, hence the name. Caccia Nanza is a specialty of Castel di Lama in the Marches. This is the only garlic bread I have ever eaten in Italy," Mr. Giobbi concludes. It is perfectly delicious, I might add. It's good with antipasti, or pasta, and the rather flat loaf may be cut in wedges or broken off in pieces.

[1 round loaf]

2½ cups all-purpose flour
½ teaspoon salt
¾ teaspoon active dry yeast
1 cup warm water (100° to 115°, approximately)
2 cloves garlic, thinly sliced
2 tablespoons rosemary
3 tablespoons olive oil
Salt and freshly ground black pepper to taste

"Preheat the oven to 400°.

"Combine the flour, salt, yeast, and water in a mixing bowl. Blend well, then turn the dough onto a lightly floured board. Knead well, for about 15 minutes, and shape the dough into a ball. Place it in a lightly greased mixing bowl. Cover with a towel and let rise in a warm place until double its size, about 1 to 1½ hours.

"Turn the dough onto the board and knead once more. Put it back into the bowl and let rise again. Then punch down the dough and turn it onto a lightly floured board. Roll it out to ½-inch thickness. Rub the surface of a baking sheet with oil. Transfer the round of dough to a baking sheet. Make indentations over the surface of the dough and insert a

rolling dough over rolling pin
to lift onto baking sheet

thin sliver of garlic and a bit of rosemary into each indentation. Pour the olive oil over the pizza and rub gently with the hands. Sprinkle with salt and pepper and bake 15 minutes or until golden brown. Remove the garlic before serving. Serves 4 to 6."

inserting garlic slivers

Gluten Bread

Gluten bread is not only low in calories, it is also a dietetic bread for those suffering with diabetes and other illnesses. Making it is a fascinating lesson in what gluten does: the dough will resist you when you knead, will try to contract when you spread it out, but the resulting loaf is worth the battle.

It is sometimes difficult to find gluten flour—which is very high in protein, fairly high in carbohydrates, and very low in fat—but you are most apt to find it in health food shops.

[1 loaf]

1 package active dry yeast
1 cup plus 2 tablespoons warm water
  (100° to 115°, approximately)
2⅓ cups gluten flour
1 teaspoon salt
1 egg white, beaten with 1 tablespoon water

◄? Allow the yeast to dissolve in the 2 tablespoons warm water, and when it begins to proof combine it with the additional cup of water. Stir in the flour and salt and knead thoroughly for 10 to 15 minutes. Roll the dough out and form into a loaf; it won't be easy. Place firmly in a well-buttered 8 x 4 x 2-inch pan, and allow it to rise until doubled in bulk. Brush with the egg wash and slash the top of the loaf twice. Bake in a preheated oven at 350° for 50 to 60 minutes, until the loaf is nicely browned and sounds hollow top and bottom when tapped with the knuckles. Cool on a rack before slicing.

Plain Saffron Bread

This bread is reminiscent of Cornish and Welsh teas, where saffron buns and bread have been exceedingly popular for generations. If one is fond of the color and the rather unusual flavor of saffron, this loaf is a happy change from traditional breads. It is rather light in texture, distinctive in flavor, and a deep orangey yellow, streaked with the tiny stigmas of the crocus that make saffron. It makes fine toast.

[2 loaves]

½ teaspoon saffron threads
⅓ cup boiling water
1 package active dry yeast
2 tablespoons granulated sugar
½ cup warm water (100° to 115°, approximately)
1 scant cup evaporated milk
1 tablespoon butter
1 heaping teaspoon salt
4 to 5 cups all-purpose flour, more if necessary

◄⅔Pour the boiling water over the saffron and steep 5 minutes. Cool and reserve. Mix the yeast and sugar in the ½ cup warm water and let proof. Scald the milk and add the butter and salt. Cool. Combine these three mixtures and blend well. Add the flour, 1 cup at a time, and beat hard with a wooden spoon. Use enough flour to make a stiff, sticky dough. Turn the dough out on a lightly floured surface and knead until smooth and elastic. Shape the dough into a ball, put in a buttered bowl, and turn to coat the surface with butter. Cover, set in a warm, draft-free place, and let rise until doubled in bulk. Punch down, turn out, and knead for another minute. Put back in the bowl to rise again until doubled in bulk. Punch down, shape into two loaves, and put in buttered 8 x 4 x 2-inch loaf tins. Cover and let rise to double in bulk again. Bake in a preheated oven at 425° for 10 minutes, then lower the temperature to 350° and continue baking for 20 to 25 minutes more, until the crust is a dark, lustrous color and the bread sounds hollow when rapped on top and bottom with the knuckles. Cool on racks before serving.

VARIATION

• **Saffron Fruit Bread:** Adding eggs, more sugar, spices, and fruits converts this into a tea bread. Excellent thinly sliced and buttered, it is also extraordinarily good for toast. Its festive character makes it a pleasant bread to give away during the holidays.

[2 loaves or 12 buns]

Use the ingredients listed in the master recipe, plus the following:
2 eggs
½ cup granulated sugar
2 teaspoons ground cinnamon
1 teaspoon grated nutmeg
1 teaspoon ground cloves
½ cup chopped currants
½ cup chopped citron
1 tablespoon caraway seeds

◄? Add the eggs, additional sugar, and spices to the dough before first kneading, plus additional flour if needed to compensate for the eggs. After the first rising, knead in the currants, citron, and caraway seeds lightly dusted with flour. Proceed as in the master recipe, except that you will use 9 x 5 x 3 pans. The dough can also be shaped into buns, placed on greased baking sheets, and allowed to rise until almost doubled in bulk. Bake at 400° for approximately 20 to 25 minutes.

Italian Feather Bread

This is a very easy-to-make, light, fluffy, and flavorful loaf, a bread to eat while still warm. It's excellent with summer fare—cold meats, salads, and vegetables—or merely with coffee and preserves.

[2 free-form loaves]

2 packages active dry yeast
1 tablespoon granulated sugar
1 cup warm water (100° to 115°, approximately)
⅓ cup butter, cut into small pieces
¾ cup hot water
2 teaspoons salt
5½ to 6 cups all-purpose flour
Cornmeal
1 egg white, lightly beaten

◄₹Stir the yeast, sugar, and warm water together in a large mixing bowl; let sit till yeast dissolves and starts to proof. In the meantime, melt the butter in the hot water and let cool to lukewarm. Add the salt, and combine with the yeast mixture. Stirring vigorously with a wooden spoon, add the flour, 1 cup at a time, until the dough almost comes away from the sides of the bowl. (Don't be afraid if it seems rather soft and sticky; it will stabilize in the next step.) Turn out the dough onto a lightly floured board. Using a baker's scraper or large spatula, scrape under the flour and dough, fold the dough over, and press it with your free hand. Continue until the dough has absorbed enough flour from the board and is easy to handle. Knead for 2 to 4 minutes, being sure to keep your hands well floured, because it is still a sticky dough. When the dough is soft and smooth, let rest for 5 or 6 minutes and then divide in two. Roll each half into a rectangle about 12 inches long and 8 inches wide (see page 32). Starting from the wide end, roll this up quite tightly, pinching the seams as you roll.

Butter one or two baking sheets well and sprinkle with cornmeal. Place the loaves on the sheets, and let them rise in a warm, draft-free place until doubled in bulk, about 50 to 60 minutes. Brush with beaten egg white and bake in a preheated 425° oven 40 minutes, or until the loaves are a rich, golden color and make a hollow sound when you tap the crust, top and bottom, with your knuckles. Cool on a rack and slice when quite fresh.

Salt-Rising Bread

Salt-rising bread is one of the oldest breads in this country. It has a delicious and unusual flavor and a very smooth texture. In fact, it is one of the most remarkable of all breads. It does present one great difficulty for the breadmaker. It is unpredictable. You may try the same recipe without success three or four times and find that it works the fifth time. Or you may get a loaf that is halfway good. If it works, fine; if it doesn't, forget it. I am including it in this collection because it is a worthy recipe, but I do so with a warning that you may be disappointed.

To keep the starter at a steady temperature, which the recipe requires, leave it in an electric oven with the light on—this will provide just enough warmth—or in a gas oven with the pilot light on. In the old days it used to be kept in hot water for 25 hours, the bowl covered with quilts. The foam that forms may not be one, two, or three inches in thickness, but if it foams at all make the loaf and see what happens. Good luck!

[2 loaves]

FOR THE SALT-RISING STARTER:
1½ cups hot water
1 medium potato, peeled and sliced thin
2 tablespoons white or yellow cornmeal
1 teaspoon granulated sugar
½ teaspoon salt

◄₂ Mix the starter ingredients and pour into a 2-quart jar or deep bowl that has been rinsed well with hot water. Cover with a lid or plate. Put the jar into a larger bowl or pan and surround with boiling water. Cover the large bowl with plastic or a towel, and cover this with three or four towels or a blanket. It should stand at a temperature of 100 degrees when the mixture is finally foaming. The electric oven turned to warm will provide the right temperature, and so will a gas range with a pilot light on. In either case, let the starter stand about 12 hours, or until the top is covered with ½ to 1 inch of foam. Sometimes it will take longer to foam, even 24 hours, but continue to keep it warm.

FOR THE BREAD:
Liquid from starter (see above)
½ cup warm water (100° to 115°, approximately)
¼ teaspoon baking soda
½ cup undiluted evaporated milk
    or ½ cup lukewarm whole milk
1 tablespoon melted butter
1 teaspoon salt
4½ to 5½ cups all-purpose
    or hard-wheat flour

◄᠈Let the liquid from the potato drip through a strainer into a mix-ing bowl, and then pour the warm water through the potatoes, pressing out as much liquid as possible. Discard the potatoes. Add to the drained liquid the soda, milk, melted butter, and salt, mixing well. Stir in 2 cups of the flour and beat until very smooth. Stir in the remaining flour, a cup at a time, until a soft dough is formed, using up to 4½ cups. Put a cup of flour on the bread board and turn the dough onto it. Sprinkle a little of the flour on top of the dough and knead lightly for 10 to 12 minutes, or until the dough is smooth but still soft. Divide the dough and shape into two loaves (this bread does not have a rising between the kneading and the shaping). Place in well-buttered bread pans, brush the top of each loaf with melted butter, cover, and place in a warm, draft-free place to rise until doubled in bulk. (This will take longer than regular bread—as long as 4 to 5 hours, maybe more.) Bake in a preheated oven at 375° for 35 to 45 minutes, or until the loaves shrink from the sides of the pans. Remove from pans to cool.

Sourdough Bread

Despite my own feeling that sourdough bread is much overrated and is difficult to perfect at home, I am including one recipe in this collection because interest in the subject is so tremendous. This recipe came to me from Jeanne Voltz, the former food editor of the *Los Angeles Times*, who worked with sourdough over a period of years in California, where it has long been popular. Jeanne agrees with me that it is a most fickle process. I have found, for example, that the starter can react differently within the same region. In New York City I never had the success with it that I had in Connecticut or Long Island or Massachusetts. I have even found variations in its performance from one neighborhood of New York to another. Certainly it is just as unpredictable as Salt-Rising Bread (page 68), and I am not sure it is worth the trouble. I would much rather have you spend your time producing the Buttermilk White Bread (page 42) or some of the rye breads. But for those who like a challenge, here it is:

[2 long or 2 regular loaves]

FOR THE STARTER:

1 cup milk
1 cup water
1 tablespoon granulated sugar
1 teaspoon salt
2 cups all-purpose flour
1 package active dry yeast
½ cup warm water (100° to 115°, approximately)

FOR THE SPONGE:

1 cup warm water
1 cup starter (see above)
2 teaspoons granulated sugar
2 teaspoons salt
4 cups all-purpose flour

FOR THE BREAD:

1 package active dry yeast
½ cup warm water (100° to 115°, approximately)
Sourdough sponge (see above)
1½ to 2½ cups all-purpose flour

◄ɜTo begin preparation of the starter, heat the milk, add the water, and cool to lukewarm. Stir in the sugar, salt, and flour, and beat until well blended. Turn into a large crock, allowing ample room for expansion. Cover with a cloth or cheesecloth and let stand in a warm place 3 to 5 days, or until the mixture is bubbly and has a sour aroma (if it really takes, it can drive you right out of the room). Dissolve the yeast in the ½ cup warm water and beat into the starter. Cover with a damp cloth and let stand at room temperature for a week, stirring down each day. (It will continue to smell to high heaven, I warn you.) If it separates, don't worry; stir. At the end of the week remove the cloth and cover the crock with a lid. Your starter is now ready to use.

The night before, or several hours before baking, combine the ingredients for the sponge and beat with a wooden spoon to blend well. Cover with foil or plastic wrap and allow to stand at room temperature until doubled in bulk. Then begin the actual preparation of the bread.

Soften the yeast in the warm water in a large bowl. Add the sourdough sponge, and stir in about 1 cup flour. Turn out on a floured board and knead in additional flour to make a very stiff dough. Place in a buttered bowl, turning the dough to coat the surface with butter. Cover and let rise in a warm place until doubled in bulk, 1½ to 2 hours.

Punch the dough down, return to the bowl, and let rise once more for 45 minutes. Turn out on a lightly floured surface and divide the dough in half. Shape each half into a French-type loaf or a loaf to be fitted into a 9 x 5 x 3-inch bread pan. If making the French-type loaf, place on a baking sheet that has been sprinkled with cornmeal and slash the loaves 3 or 4 times across the top with a razor blade or a sharp knife. If using bread pans, butter them and fit the loaves into them. Allow the loaves to rise in a warm, draft-free spot for 1 hour. Preheat the oven to 400°, and place a shallow pan of boiling water on the lowest rack. Place the bread on the rack above or on a rack lined with heated tiles (see page 12). Bake for 35 to 40 minutes, or until the bread sounds hollow when tapped with the knuckles. Cool on a rack before slicing.

NOTE

As you use the starter, always replenish it by stirring in, for each ½ cup removed, ½ cup flour and ½ cup lukewarm water. Even if no starter is used, it should be stirred once a day and the ½ cup flour and ½ cup lukewarm water added once a week. If the room temperature is above 85°, store the starter in the refrigerator. Also refrigerate it if you do not use it every 2 or 3 days.

WHOLE-MEAL BREADS

Myrtle Allen's Brown Bread

I first ate Myrtle Allen's brown bread in her delightful inn, Bally-maloe House, in Ireland. It is an uncommonly well-textured whole-wheat bread with a lovely flavor, and I have made it repeatedly since visiting there. It should be eaten fresh, with plenty of good sweet butter. You will note that this is an unusual recipe, since the dough is not kneaded and has only one rising.

[1 loaf]

    3¾ cup whole-wheat flour,
      preferably stone ground
    1½ packages active dry yeast
    2 cups warm water (100° to 115°, approximately)
    2 tablespoons molasses
    1 tablespoon salt

◄¿Put the whole-wheat flour in a large mixing bowl and place in a warm oven (a gas oven with the pilot light on or an electric oven set as low as possible). Both the flour and the bowl should be warm when you make the bread.

Dissolve the yeast in ½ cup of the warm water, and blend in the molasses. Let proof. Add another ½ cup of water. Combine the flour, yeast mixture, and salt. Add enough warm water to make a wet, sticky dough (about 1 cup or more according to the flour). Put directly into a buttered 9 x 5 x 3-inch bread tin. Cover, set in a warm spot, allow to rise by one-third its original size. Preheat the oven and bake at 450° for 50

risen loaf in pan

minutes, or until the crust is nicely browned and the loaf sounds hollow when tapped. Remove from the pan and leave on the rack in the turned-off oven for 20 minutes more to give a crustier finish.

Whole-Wheat Bread Made with Hard-Wheat Flour

You must get the specially milled hard-wheat and whole-wheat flour for this bread. It is as good a coarse-meal bread as I know, and has a lovely smell when baking and cooling. If you prefer, you may substitute honey for molasses.

[1 large free-form loaf or 2 regular loaves]

2 packages active dry yeast
1 tablespoon granulated sugar
2 cups warm water (100° to 115°, approximately)
¼ cup melted butter
2 tablespoons molasses
1½ tablespoons salt
3 cups whole-wheat flour
2 cups hard-wheat flour
1 egg beaten with 1 teaspoon water

◄Dissolve the yeast and sugar in ½ cup of the warm water in a large mixing bowl and let proof for 5 minutes. Stir the butter into the remaining 1½ cups warm water; add the molasses and salt. Add this mixture to the yeast mixture and blend with a wooden spoon, then add the whole-wheat flour, 1 cup at a time, beating hard after each addition. Stir in 1½ cups of hard-wheat flour. When the dough gets too stiff and sticky to work, turn it out on a board sprinkled with about ½ cup hard-wheat flour and knead a good 10 minutes, or until the dough is smooth and pliable. (It may retain a bit of stickiness, as do most doughs made with dark-wheat flours.) Shape into a ball, place in a well-buttered bowl, and turn to coat with the butter. Cover, set in a warm, draft-free spot, and let rise until doubled in bulk, about 1 hour, possibly longer.

Punch down, and if you want 2 loaves, divide in two and shape each piece into a loaf to fit an 8 x 4 x 2 or 9 x 5 x 3-inch loaf tin. Or make

egg wash

one large free-form loaf. Cover and let rise again until doubled in bulk. Brush the loaves with the egg wash. Bake in a preheated 425° oven for 10 minutes, then lower the temperature to 375° and continue to bake for 20 to 25 minutes longer, until crust is glazed and the bread sounds hollow when removed from tins and tapped on top and bottom.

William Melville Childs' Health Bread

This unusual bread recipe was sent me by a dear friend and great cook, Janet Wurtzburger, who is compiling a benefit cookbook for the Walters Art Gallery in Baltimore. It was perfected by a Marylander whose name is William Melville Childs. A veteran breadmaker, Mr. Childs grinds his own whole-wheat flour and recommends that you do the same. Buy whole-wheat berries (not chemically treated, but suitable for human diet), and grind them with a little hand mill or in an electric blender. This produces a very coarse meal, which is what Mr. Childs prefers in the bread. His variation on this recipe, which follows, uses absolutely no white flour and has a somewhat denser texture, but also more flavor.

[2 loaves]

2 packages active dry yeast
¾ cup warm milk (100° to 115°, approximately)
1 teaspoon granulated sugar, more or less to taste
2¼ cups boiling water
2 cups quick-cooking oats
3½ cups whole-wheat flour,
 either 100% whole-wheat graham or
 hand-milled whole wheat
¾ cup dark molasses
1½ tablespoons butter or margarine
1 tablespoon salt
3½ cups all-purpose flour

◀ᶾDissolve the yeast in the warm milk and add the sugar. Let the yeast proof. In a large mixing bowl pour boiling water over the oatmeal and whole wheat (only if you are using home-ground whole-wheat flour; if using commercially ground, add it later, with the all-purpose flour), and stir well. Allow to cool to about 98°. Warm the molasses, butter, and salt together in a saucepan, and add to the grain mixture. Then add the milk-yeast mixture, and stir with a heavy spoon or wooden spatula. Gradually add the all-purpose flour, reserving 1 cup for kneading, and if you have not used home-ground whole wheat, also add the whole-wheat flour. Mix this in very, very well with your hands because it is going to be a heavy dough. Cover with a cloth, place in a warm, draft-free spot or over hot water, and allow to rise until doubled in bulk. Remove to a floured board and knead lightly, using additional flour if the dough seems sticky. Continue to knead until the dough is smooth and satiny, about 10 to 12 minutes. Divide into two pieces, form two loaves, and place in 9 x 5 x 3-inch buttered pans. Again let dough rise in a warm spot, until doubled in bulk. Bake in a 350° oven for 1 hour. Remove the loaves from the pans and place them back in the oven to dry out slightly. Then cool on racks.

VARIATION

2 packages active dry yeast
1⅛ cups warm milk (100° to 115°, approximately)
1 teaspoon granulated sugar

1⅞ cups boiling water
4 cups quick-cooking oats
5 cups whole-wheat flour, either
    home ground or the commercial 100%
¾ cup dark molasses
1½ tablespoons butter or margarine
2¼ teaspoons to 1 tablespoon salt

◄3 Proceed exactly as directed in the master recipe. The kneading will be more difficult, and the bread will not be quite as smooth. However, it is an interesting, pleasant tasting loaf.

Norwegian Whole-Wheat Bread

Taught in the Norwegian Government School for Domestic Science Teachers in Oslo, this recipe makes a very dense, coarse bread full of honest flavor, and it slices nicely. The dough will be stiff and difficult to knead, but I am sure you will find the results worth your labors.

[2 free-form loaves]

2 packages active dry yeast
4 cups warm milk (100° to 115°, approximately)
8 cups whole-wheat flour
2 cups fine rye flour
2 cups unbleached all-purpose flour
1-2 tablespoons salt
Cornmeal

In a large mixing bowl dissolve the yeast in ½ cup of the warm milk. Allow to proof. Add the remaining milk, and gradually beat or stir in the three flours and the salt to make a firm dough. Remove the dough to a well-floured board and knead 10 to 12 minutes. (It is going to be hard to work, as I have warned.) When you have a satiny, elastic dough, form it into a ball. Place in a well-buttered bowl, and turn to coat the surface. Cover and set in a warm spot to rise until doubled in bulk.

Punch the dough down, turn out on a floured board, and knead again for 2 or 3 minutes. Cut into two equal pieces. Sprinkle one very large baking sheet or two small ones with a bit of cornmeal. Shape the dough into round loaves, and place them on the baking sheet or sheets. Cover and let rise in a warm place until almost doubled in bulk, which will take as long as 2 hours, because this is a firm-textured bread. (I like to slash a cross in the loaves before baking, which allows them to rise more freely and gives them a handsome look.) Bake in a preheated oven at 375° degrees for about an hour, or until the loaves sound hollow when you tap them with your knuckles. Cool thoroughly before slicing. This bread cuts beautifully and will remain fresh for quite a while if wrapped in a towel or placed in a plastic bag in the refrigerator.

Whole-Meal Bread with Potatoes

Well worth recording here, this is another of the recipes provided by the Norwegian Government School for Domestic Science Teachers. The potatoes help the bread to rise and give it a wonderful, moist texture. It's an altogether marvelous loaf.

[2 round loaves]

2 packages active dry yeast
½ cup warm water (100° to 115°, approximately)
1 pound potatoes (about 2 medium),
    peeled and grated
3 cups buttermilk
1-2 tablespoons salt
6 cups whole-meal whole-wheat flour
4 cups all-purpose flour
Cornmeal (optional)

◄ Proof the yeast in the warm water. Heat the potatoes in a heavy saucepan, with a small amount of the buttermilk, till lukewarm, then add to the yeast mixture. Then add the salt and the remainder of the buttermilk, which should also be heated until a little more than lukewarm. With your hand or a wooden spoon stir in the 10 cups of flour, a cup at a time, until you have a very firm dough. Knead until elastic and shiny, about 10 to 12 minutes, then place in a well-buttered bowl and turn to coat the surface with the butter. Cover, set in a warm, draft-free spot, and let rise until doubled in bulk.

Punch the dough down and knead again for 3 or 4 minutes. Shape into two round, cottage-type loaves, and place on baking sheets that have been buttered or sprinkled with a little cornmeal. Let them rise until doubled in bulk, then bake in a preheated oven at 375° for at least 30 to 35 minutes, or until the loaves sound hollow when rapped on top and bottom. Cool on racks before slicing.

Cracked-Wheat Bread

This is an interesting, crunchy, rather solid bread. It has a good moist crumb and keeps well. I particularly like it toasted and well buttered, and I find it pleasing for certain sandwiches.

[2 loaves]

½ cup fine cracked wheat
1½ cups boiling water
1 package active dry yeast
⅓ cup warm water (100° to 115°, approximately)
¼ cup softened butter or shortening
1½ tablespoons salt
2 tablespoons molasses
2 tablespoons honey
1 cup milk
1 cup whole-wheat flour
4 cups all-purpose flour

❧ Cook the cracked wheat in the boiling water about 10 minutes, stirring occasionally to prevent sticking, until all the water is absorbed. Dissolve the yeast in the ⅓ cup lukewarm water in a large mixing bowl and let proof. Stir the butter, salt, molasses, honey, and milk into the cooked cracked wheat. Cool to lukewarm, then add to the yeast mixture. With a large spoon or with one hand, start stirring in the flours, 1 cup at a time. When the dough is stiff enough to work, turn out on a floured board and knead a good 10 to 12 minutes, working in a little of the remaining flour as necessary. (The dough will retain a slightly tacky but not sticky texture.) When smooth and elastic, shape into a ball and put in a buttered bowl, turning to coat with butter. Cover, place in a warm, draft-free spot, and let rise until doubled in bulk, about 1½ hours. Punch down and shape into two loaves. Put in well-buttered 9 x 5 x 3-inch loaf pans, cover, and let rise again until doubled in bulk, or until the dough reaches the tops of the pans. Bake in a preheated 375° oven 30 to 35 minutes, or until the loaves sound hollow when tapped on top and bottom. Cool on racks.

Mrs. Elizabeth Ovenstad's Bread

I learned to make this bread in Norway, at Mrs. Ovenstad's farm near Oslo. She bakes it twice a week, and though she resorts to heating the dough over steam for the second rising, it comes out beautifully. She is also a deft pastry cook and gardener, and loves to eat.

[2 large loaves]

2 cups boiling water
⅔ cup whole-wheat kernels (available in
    health food stores)
2 packages active dry yeast
1 tablespoon granulated sugar
½ cup warm water (100° to 115°, approximately)
½ cup rye flour
½ cup whole-meal whole-wheat flour
8 cups all-purpose flour, preferably unbleached
1 tablespoon salt
3 cups milk and water, mixed approximately
    half and half

◄᠊ Pour the boiling water over the whole-wheat kernels and let stand for an hour or two to soften. Proof the yeast and sugar together in the warm water. Combine the rye, whole-wheat, and white flours with the salt and blend well. Add the yeast mixture, the drained whole-wheat kernels, and the milk-water; knead well for 10 to 15 minutes. (Or use the electric mixer, if you have a heavy-duty model with a dough hook, and blend thoroughly.) Form the dough into a ball, and place in a well-buttered bowl, turning the dough to coat all sides. Cover and let rise in a warm, draft-free place for about 1 hour. When it has risen to almost double its bulk, punch down and remove to a floured board. Knead about 10 minutes, then cut into two equal pieces. Knead each piece lightly, and form into a loaf to fit a 10 x 5 x 3-inch bread pan; or form loaves about 16 inches long and 4 inches wide and fit side by side in a pan about an inch deep. Cover and allow the dough to rise again until almost doubled in bulk, then brush with butter or water and slash each loaf two or three times with a very sharp knife or a razor blade. Bake in a preheated 400° oven for approximately 1 hour, or until the loaves sound hollow when tapped on top and bottom. (This bread should have a good crunchy crust, so a few moments extra cooking will not hurt it.) Remove to a rack and allow to cool before cutting.

NOTES

1. If whole-wheat kernels are not available, you can substitute ⅔ cup of Ralston or other whole-wheat cereal.

2. If you want to do the second rising quickly, as Mrs. Ovenstad did, place the pan of dough over a steaming pot of water. It will not harm the dough in any way or affect its final texture.

Graham Bread

An old recipe that I have used for many years, this makes a very nicely textured, flavorful, and interesting bread. Good baked either in loaf tins or in a free-form oval loaf, slashed with a sharp knife before baking, it is an excellent sandwich bread and a good toaster. This is a large recipe, but the bread lasts exceedingly well (and of course can be frozen); the recipe can be cut in half successfully.

[2 or 3 loaves]

2 packages active dry yeast
3 tablespoons granulated sugar
2 cups warm water (100° to 115°, approximately)
1 thirteen-ounce can evaporated milk
¼ cup melted butter
2 tablespoons salt
3 cups graham flour
5 to 6 cups all-purpose flour

◆ Dissolve the yeast and sugar in ½ cup of water in a large bowl and let proof for about 5 minutes. Combine the evaporated milk and the remaining 1½ cups water, and heat to warm. Remove from the heat and add butter and salt. Add this mixture to the yeast mixture, and blend well with a wooden spoon. Add the 3 cups of graham flour to the liquids and beat hard with the spoon or with your hand. Stir in about 3 cups of the all-purpose flour, 1 cup at a time, and beat well. (The dough will become sticky and the flour will be hard to incorporate.) Add enough of the remaining flour to make a firm dough, and beat until it comes away from the sides of the bowl. Turn out on a lightly floured board, and knead, using the remaining flour, until it is smooth and elastic, which will take a good 7 to 10 minutes. Shape into a ball, put into a buttered bowl, and turn to coat with butter on all sides. Cover and allow to rest in a warm, draft-free place until doubled in bulk.

Punch the dough down and divide into three pieces. Thoroughly butter three 9 x 5 x 3-inch loaf tins, or two 10 x 5 x 3-inch tins. Shape the dough into loaves, arrange in the tins, cover, and let rise again until doubled in bulk. Bake in a preheated 425° oven for 10 minutes, then lower the temperature to 350° and continue baking 30 to 35 minutes, or until the loaves sound hollow when removed from the pans and tapped on top and bottom with the knuckles. Cool completely on racks before slicing.

Sourdough Rye

This sourdough rye appeared in the columns of *The New York Times* several years ago. I tried it, made some changes in it, and discovered that it was one of the best recipes I have ever used. The bread has a nice crumb, slices well, and keeps extremely well. I enjoy it for sandwiches and find that, thinly sliced and well buttered, it's delicious served with smoked fish and oysters or other shellfish. The recipe is large, but in this instance I find it works better with the larger amounts, particularly since you have to prepare a starter beforehand. And, of course, if the bread is too much for your larder you can freeze some of it.

[2 free-form loaves]

2 packages active dry yeast
3¼ cups warm water (100° to 115°, approximately)
6 cups all-purpose flour, approximately
2 cups rye flour
2 teaspoons salt
1 tablespoon caraway seeds
1½ teaspoons poppy seeds
2 tablespoons melted butter
3 tablespoons granulated sugar
Cornmeal
1 egg, lightly beaten with 1 tablespoon water

Four days ahead of breadmaking, prepare the "starter." Combine 1 package of the yeast, 2 cups warm water, and 2 cups all-purpose flour in a plastic bowl or container. Cover tightly and let stand at room temperature for 2 days. Then refrigerate for at least another day (see note below).

The day before preparing the dough, combine 1 cup of starter, the rye flour, and 1 cup warm water in a bowl. Cover with plastic wrap and let stand at room temperature overnight. The next day stir down the dough and add the second package of yeast, dissolved in ¼ cup warm water, salt, caraway seeds, poppy seeds, butter, and sugar. Then add up to 4 cups all-purpose flour, 1 cup at a time, to make a stiff but workable dough. Knead for 10 to 12 minutes, then shape into a ball. Place in a buttered bowl, turning to coat the dough with the butter. Cover and let rise in a warm, draft-free place until doubled in bulk, about 2 hours.

Punch down and divide the dough in half. Shape into two round loaves and place on buttered baking sheets generously sprinkled with cornmeal. Cover and let rise again until doubled in bulk, about 1 hour. Brush with the egg wash, and bake in a preheated 375° oven for 30 minutes, or until lightly browned and the loaves sound hollow when rapped with the knuckles. Cool, covered with towels to prevent the crust from hardening.

NOTE

This will provide more starter than you need for this recipe. To keep it going, replenish with equal parts of warm water and flour, let stand again at room temperature, and then refrigerate. Continue the process each time you use some of it.

Rye Bread

A pleasant rye bread of good texture and interesting flavor. It is rather difficult to make but worth the trouble. This recipe makes two loaves in 8½ x 4½ x 2½-inch pans; or if the dough seems firm enough, it can be baked in one or two free-form loaves, in which case I would suggest letting the formed loaves rise and then very carefully inverting them (right onto hot tiles, if you have them) just before they are baked. This gives a better finished loaf.

[2 free-form or regular loaves]

1 package active dry yeast
3 tablespoons honey
¼ cup warm water (100° to 115°, approximately)
1 cup warm milk combined with ½ cup hot water
2 tablespoons softened butter
1 heaping tablespoon salt
1 tablespoon caraway seeds
2½ cups rye flour
3 cups all-purpose flour, or more if needed
¼ cup cornmeal
1 egg white, beaten lightly with 2 tablespoons water

Dissolve the yeast and honey in the warm water, and allow the mixture to proof for 4 or 5 minutes. Combine the warm milk and hot water with the softened butter and add to the yeast mixture along with the salt and caraway seeds. Add the flour, 1 cup at a time, stirring well after each addition. When you have added about 4½ cups the dough will become difficult to stir and will be quite sticky, but continue to add the remaining flour a tablespoon at a time. Scrape out the dough onto a floured board, and using a baker's scraper or a large metal spatula, scrape under the dough and flour and fold the dough over. Continue to lift and fold, and with your free hand start pressing down and away from you on these folded areas, adding more flour as needed to dust your hands and to sprinkle the board. After 2 or 3 minutes of this procedure you can eliminate the scraper. Flour both hands and knead for about 10 minutes, until the dough is soft, velvety, and elastic.

Shape the dough into a ball and place in a well-buttered bowl, turning to coat with the butter. Cover with plastic wrap and place in a warm, draft-free area to double in bulk, which will take from 1 to 2 hours. Punch down, turn out on a lightly floured board, and divide into two equal pieces. Let the dough rest 2 or 3 minutes, and then shape into two loaves, either free form or for well-buttered 8 x 4 x 2-inch loaf pans. If you are making free-form loaves allow them to rise, covered, on a buttered baking sheet sprinkled with cornmeal until almost doubled in size, and then quickly invert them and brush with the egg white and water mixture. Otherwise, let the loaves rise, covered, in their pans until they have doubled in bulk and then brush the tops with the egg white and water mixture. Bake at 400° from 45 to 50 minutes or until the loaves sound hollow when tapped with the knuckles. Cool thoroughly on racks before slicing.

Finnish Sour Rye Bread

I find this fine-grained, well-flavored rye bread a pleasant change from other breads in its category. I enjoy it sliced paper-thin for sandwiches, such as cheese or smoked meats and fish, and I find it a delicious bread for toast. It is an excellent accompaniment to meals planned with Scandinavian overtones.

[2 free-form loaves]

3½ cups rye flour
3 cups warm water, flat beer, buttermilk,
    or potato water
1 package active dry yeast
2 tablespoons salt
¼ cup warm water (100° to 115°, approximately)
3½ to 4 cups unbleached all-purpose flour
1 egg, lightly beaten with 1 tablespoon water

◆ᵹFour days ahead of breadmaking, prepare the "starter": Combine 1 cup of rye flour with 1 cup liquid, cover loosely, and set in a warm place. Stir once or twice each day, adding more liquid if the mixture becomes too dry. It should bubble and give off a strong odor.

When ready to prepare the dough, put the starter in a large mixing bowl, add 2 more cups of whatever liquid was used, and stir. Dissolve the yeast and salt in ¼ cup warm water, and also stir in. Then beat in the remaining rye flour and up to 4 cups of the white flour, 1 cup at a time, to make a somewhat soft, biscuit-like dough firm enough to hold its shape. It should not be too sticky. Turn out on a lightly floured board and knead until smooth and velvety, about 10 to 12 minutes.

Divide the dough into two equal parts and shape into balls. Place in two buttered bowls, turning to coat the dough with the butter. Cover and let rise in a warm place until doubled in bulk, about 1½ hours. Turn out on a floured board and shape into round loaves or into doughnut shapes. Place on a buttered baking sheet, cover, and let rise again until doubled in bulk, about 40 minutes. Bake in a preheated 400° oven about 45 minutes, or until the loaves are lightly browned and sound hollow when tapped with the knuckles. Ten minutes before the loaves are done, brush the tops with the egg wash. Cool, covered with towels to prevent the crust from hardening.

Dark Herb Bread

This makes a loaf quite firm in texture, with a delicious herby, peppery flavor that lasts. The garlic here is subtle and does not go stale, as sometimes happens in garlic bread. It is a fine loaf for sandwiches, makes fairly good toast, and is excellent sliced thin and buttered. It will keep for a week at a time.

[1 large loaf or 2 smaller loaves]

2 packages active dry yeast
1 tablespoon granulated sugar
1½ to 2 cups warm water (100° to 115°, approximately)
3 cups whole-wheat flour
1 cup rye meal
1½ cups unbleached all-purpose flour
¼ cup olive oil
1 tablespoon salt
1 teaspoon freshly ground black pepper
3 small cloves garlic, peeled
2 tablespoons parsley, finely chopped
1 teaspoon rosemary

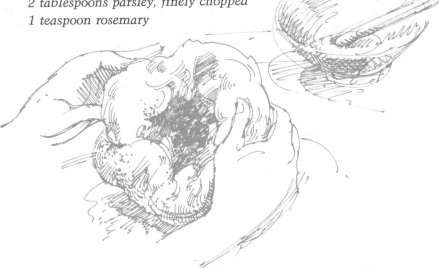

Combine the yeast, sugar, and ½ cup of the warm water in a mixing bowl and allow to proof. Mix whole-wheat flour, rye meal, and 1 cup of the all-purpose flour. Add the olive oil, salt, and pepper and mix well. Add the yeast mixture and 1 cup of warm water. Mix, adding additional water if necessary, to make a firm, slightly sticky dough. Grind the garlic, parsley, and rosemary to a paste, using a mortar and pestle. (You will have about 1 tablespoon of paste.) Work this into the dough, then turn the dough out on a floured board and knead until smooth and rather elastic, about 10 to 15 minutes, adding as much of the remaining ½ cup flour as you require. Form into a ball, place in a well-oiled bowl, and turn to coat with the oil. Cover and let rise in a warm place until doubled in bulk, about 1½ to 2 hours.

Punch the dough down and knead again for about 5 minutes, then shape into two loaves to fit well-buttered 8 x 4 x 2-inch bread tins, or make one loaf for a 10 x 5 x 3-inch tin. Cover and allow the dough to rise again until it is above the rim of the loaf tin. Slash the loaves lengthwise (or crosswise) about ½ inch deep with a knife or razor blade. Bake in a preheated oven at 400°

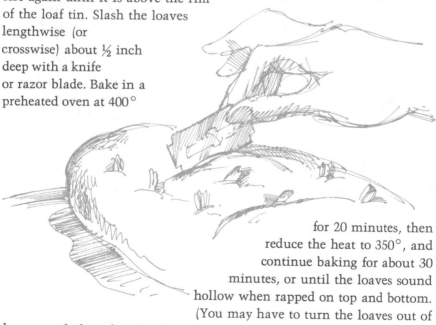

for 20 minutes, then reduce the heat to 350°, and continue baking for about 30 minutes, or until the loaves sound hollow when rapped on top and bottom. (You may have to turn the loaves out of the pan and place them back on the baking rack for a few minutes to give additional color.) Cool on racks before slicing.

NOTE

To prevent any risk of the garlic tasting a little rancid if you are keeping the loaf over a day or so, do not mix it in the bread with the herbs. Instead, cut it in very thin slices and insert into the loaf just before you put it in the oven. Then withdraw the garlic after the loaf has been baked.

VARIATION

• This herb loaf can be made using 4 cups unbleached all-purpose flour and 1 cup whole-wheat cereal. After the first rising, punch down the dough and shape into an oval or round loaf. Place on a board or cookie sheet that has been sprinkled with cornmeal and let rise to double its bulk. Just before popping it into the oven, lift carefully and invert on the baking sheet. Proceed to bake.

Pronto Pumpernickel

This was a recent winner in a breadmaking contest. It makes a delicious, moist, round loaf resembling the Middle European rye breads. It is easy to prepare, has great merit, and keeps well, too.

[1 loaf]

1 package (13¾ ounces) hot-roll mix
2 eggs, separated
¼ cup molasses
¾ cup warm water
¾ cup unsifted rye flour
1½ teaspoons caraway seed

⋙ "Prepare a hot-roll mix as directed on package, using 1 whole egg and an egg yolk, reserving the white for a glaze. Stir molasses into warm water. Then stir in the rye flour, the prepared mix, and the caraway seed. Cover and let rise in a warm, draft-free place about 45 minutes. Then punch down. Turn out on a floured board and shape into a ball. Put on a buttered baking sheet, cover, and let rise again about 45 minutes. Brush lightly with beaten egg white, and sprinkle with more caraway seed. Bake in a preheated 375° oven 35 to 40 minutes."

NOTE
If preferred, shape the bread into a loaf and put in a buttered 9 x 5 x 3-inch loaf pan, let rise, and bake as directed. Also, glaze and seed on round or loaf can be omitted.

Pumpernickel Bread I

This is an extremely interesting bread, but since it is practical to make only in large quantity, I recommend it solely to those of you who have large kitchens and large bowls. Besides this, the dough is very sticky and takes a lot of deft working to get it to the baking stage. So if you have any reservations about the challenge, I urge that you try another pumpernickel. However, this recipe can be made into a nicely workable dough, and the baked loaf has great flavor and quality.

[2 large loaves]

> 2 packages active dry yeast
> 1 tablespoon granulated sugar
> ½ cup warm water (100° to 115°, approximately)
> 1½ cups cold water
> ¾ cup cornmeal, or more if needed
> 1½ cups boiling water
> 1 tablespoon salt
> 2 tablespoons butter
> 1 tablespoon caraway seeds
> 2 cups mashed potatoes
> 4 cups rye flour
> 4 cups all-purpose flour, or
>   more if needed
> Melted butter

◄ Dissolve the yeast and sugar in the ½ cup warm water and let proof 4 or 5 minutes. Stir the cold water into ¾ cup of the cornmeal, add the boiling water, and cook over medium heat, stirring constantly, for about 2 minutes, or until thickened. Pour into a large mixing bowl. Add the salt, butter, and caraway seeds and let cool until lukewarm. Add the potatoes and yeast mixture, and then stir in the flours, 1 cup at a time, mixing well; the dough will be very sticky. Turn out on a floured board and knead for about 15 minutes, adding enough flour and cornmeal to produce a firm, evenly textured dough. (The dough will remain quite sticky and will not become very elastic, so don't be alarmed if you require more than ½ cup each of flour and cornmeal for kneading.) Shape the dough into a ball, place in a buttered bowl, and brush with melted butter. Cover with plastic wrap and let rise, in a warm, draft-free spot, until doubled in bulk.

Punch the dough down, let rest for 2 or 3 minutes, then knead again for a good 5 minutes. Let rest again, then shape into two or three loaves. Butter 10 x 4 x 3-inch or 12-inch pans, and fit the dough into them. Cover and let it rise again until doubled in bulk. Bake at 425° for about 10 minutes, then reduce the heat to 350° and continue to bake for about 40 to 50 minutes more. The loaves will get a dark crust and sound hollow when tapped on the top and bottom with the knuckles.

Rub the crusts well with butter or brush with melted butter when the bread comes out of the oven. Cool thoroughly on racks before slicing.

Pumpernickel Bread II

A good, gutsy bread with a rather dense texture, this is not the easiest bread to put together, but that is generally true of breads using a great deal of rye flour. It's worth the work. This pumpernickel is more Scandinavian than the preceding recipe, which has a Slavic accent.

[1 loaf]

> 1 package active dry yeast
> 1 tablespoon granulated sugar, raw if you prefer
> 1¼ cups warm water (100° to 115°, approximately)
> 2 tablespoons molasses
> 2 tablespoons oil or butter
> 1 tablespoon salt
> 1 cup all-purpose flour, more if necessary
> 1 cup whole-wheat flour
> 2 cups rye flour
> ½ cup cornmeal

◄ Combine the yeast, sugar, and ¼ cup warm water in a large mixing bowl, and let proof for 5 minutes. Add the molasses, the oil or butter, and salt and mix well. Add the remaining cup of water. Mix the flours and cornmeal together, and add, a cup at a time, to the yeast mixture, beating it in until you have a fairly stiff but workable dough; it will be quite sticky, heavy, and difficult to blend. Turn out on a floured board and knead, adding more flour as necessary, until the dough becomes smooth and fairly elastic. It will take at least 10 minutes of kneading and possibly longer until the dough is only slightly sticky. (It will not be completely resilient, and it is apt to remain extremely heavy.) Shape into a ball, put into a buttered bowl, and turn to coat on all sides. Cover and let rise in a warm, draft-free spot until doubled in bulk, a good 2 to 2½ hours.

Punch the dough down and shape into a loaf that will fit a well-buttered 8 x 4 x 2-inch tin. Cover and let rise to the top of the pan, another 2 to 3 hours—so be patient. Bake in a preheated 375° oven 35 to 45 minutes, or until the loaf sounds hollow when tapped on top and bottom. Cool thoroughly on a rack before slicing.

Anadama Bread

There are many recipes for this famous American loaf. No two people agree on what the original was, but it is practically certain that it contained cornmeal and molasses. I have had interesting Anadama breads made with graham flour, white flour, and cornmeal. It can also be made with brown sugar or raw sugar instead of molasses.

[1 large loaf or 2 smaller loaves]

1 package active dry yeast
1 teaspoon granulated sugar
1¼ cups warm water (100° to 115°, approximately)
2 tablespoons butter
¼ cup molasses
1 tablespoon salt
½ cup yellow cornmeal
4½ cups all-purpose flour, approximately

◄¿Dissolve the yeast and sugar in ¼ cup warm water in a large bowl and let proof for 5 minutes. Combine the remaining water, butter, molasses, and salt in a saucepan, and heat to lukewarm. Stir into the yeast mixture. Add the cornmeal and mix well. Add the flour, 1 cup at a time, and beat vigorously; the dough will be sticky and hard to work. Turn out on a lightly floured board. Using a baker's scraper or large spatula, scrape under the flour on the board and fold the dough over to incorporate the flour. Repeat this process until you can knead with your hands, using only enough additional flour to make a smooth dough that is springy to touch; the stickiness will not be completely eliminated. Shape into a ball, put in a buttered bowl, and turn to coat the surface with the fat. Cover and let rise in a warm, draft-free place until doubled in bulk.

Punch the dough down. Shape into one loaf, to fit a 10-inch loaf pan, or divide into two pieces and shape to fit two 8 x 4 x 2-inch loaf tins. Cover and let rise until doubled in bulk. Bake in a preheated 425° oven for 10 minutes, then lower the temperature to 350° and bake for about 35 minutes more, or until the loaves sound hollow when tapped with the knuckles on top and bottom. Cool on racks.

Bavarian Rye Bread

This quite unusual bread is from a very old German recipe. Originally the dough was prepared at home and put into an airtight wooden keg for 18 to 24 hours. Then it was formed into loaves and rushed to the local baker's oven. I have worked out a version that can be done from start to finish in your own kitchen. It makes a delicious loaf of bread—sturdy, close textured, and highly distinctive in flavor. It slices very thin and is excellent with cheese, cold meats, and sausages.

[1 loaf]

1 package active dry yeast
1 heaping tablespoon salt
1½ cups warm water (100° to 115°,
 approximately), or enough to make
 a heavy, pastelike dough
3¾ cups rye flour

◄⦆Combine the yeast, salt, and water in a mixing bowl. Add the flour, cup by cup, stirring with a wooden spoon to incorporate as much of it as you can. Turn out on a floured board, and knead enough to blend the ingredients. You will have a very heavy dough with little or no life, so shape it as best you can into a ball and place in a small, well-buttered bowl, turning to coat the surface with butter. Cover the bowl with plastic wrap to seal, and then cover with foil. Let rest in a semi-warm area for 16 to 18 hours.

Uncover. You will note that little or nothing has happened to the dough. Punch it down anyway, and knead it on a lightly floured board for a minute or two. (You'll find it easier to handle than the original mass.) Butter an 8 x 4 x 2-inch loaf tin and shape the dough to fit it. Cover and let rise in a warm, draft-free spot until doubled in bulk.

Bake in a preheated 375° oven 45 to 50 minutes, or until the bread sounds hollow when tapped on top and bottom. The finished loaf will be about 2½ inches high.

Black Bread

There are numerous varieties of what is known as "black bread." I tried out recipes for a great many in the course of this book and finally settled on this one, which is not as dark as the commercial ones but has a flavor that I think is extraordinarily good and a very nice texture. It is rather fun to make, too, and even if you don't achieve the perfect look that one finds in the professional loaves of this kind, the recipe works very well. Thinly sliced it is a delicious bread with seafood, and it makes extremely good sandwiches. It will hold well if wrapped in plastic wrap and kept in the refrigerator. It has the advantage over many other black breads of not being too sweet.

[2 free-form or regular loaves]

⅜ cup cornmeal
¾ cup cold water
¾ cup boiling water
1 tablespoon butter
1 tablespoon salt
2 tablespoons and 1 teaspoon brown sugar
1½ teaspoons caraway seeds
1 tablespoon unsweetened cocoa
1 tablespoon instant coffee
2 packages active dry yeast
¼ cup warm water (100° to 115°, approximately)
2 cups rye (dark) flour
1 cup whole-wheat flour
2 cups unbleached all-purpose flour
Additional flour for kneading
1 egg white beaten with 2 tablespoons water

◦⟩ Add the cornmeal to the cold water and mix well. Pour into boiling water and stir until thickened. When it is thickened and bubbly, stir in the butter, salt, sugar, caraway seeds, cocoa, and instant coffee.

Dissolve the yeast in warm water, add to the mixture, and stir well.

Blend in the flours, adding more liquid if necessary, and stir until you have a fairly sticky dough. Turn out on a floured board and knead, adding more flour if necessary, to make a firm, elastic dough. Form into a ball and place in a well-buttered bowl, turning to coat with butter on all sides. Put in a warm, draft-free spot to rise until doubled in bulk. Punch down the dough and knead for two or three minutes. Form into two balls, and either shape into free-form loaves or roll and fit into two bread pans 8 x 4 x 2 inches. Allow to rise until almost doubled in bulk. Brush the bread with the beaten egg white and cold water and bake at 375° for 50 to 60 minutes or until the bread taps hollow. If you have doubts about whether it is done, let it bake longer. This loaf is better a little overdone than underdone.

NOTE

If the bread is to be baked in round free-form loaves, arrange on a baking sheet sprinkled with cornmeal and place a flan ring or other guard around the dough to prevent its spreading too much; or let the loaves rise in 8-inch pie tins or skillets and then turn out onto the baking sheet or directly onto oven tiles (see page 12) just before baking.

Maryetta's Oatmeal Bread

This is as good an oatmeal bread as I have ever eaten, and it makes wonderful toast. The recipe yields a great deal more than the previous one, so it is good if you have a large family or want to give a loaf away as a gift. It is essential to leave the dough uncovered during the two risings.

[3 loaves]

4 cups boiling water
3 cups rolled oats
7½ to 8 cups all-purpose flour,
    approximately, preferably unbleached
2 packages active dry yeast
2 tablespoons salt
4 tablespoons salad oil
½ cup molasses

◄ᴣPour the boiling water over the oatmeal in a large bowl and leave to cool. Then stir in 2 cups of flour and the yeast. Place in a warm, draft-free spot and allow to rise, uncovered, until doubled in bulk. Punch down and work in the salt, salad oil, molasses, and enough of the remaining flour to make a stiff dough. Turn out on a floured board and knead, adding extra flour if necessary, to make a smooth, pliable, firm dough—about 10 minutes, but you cannot knead too much. Divide the dough into three equal pieces, and form into loaves to fit three buttered 9 x 5 x 3-inch loaf tins. Allow to rise again, uncovered, until doubled in bulk. Bake in a preheated 350° oven 40 to 60 minutes, or until the bread sounds hollow when removed from the tins and rapped on top and bottom. Cool on racks before slicing.

Oatmeal Bread with Cooked Oatmeal

There are two or three favorite recipes for oatmeal bread in this country. I first encountered this one in Nevada, in a restaurant that was made famous by Lucius Beebe, and it was so good that I extracted the recipe from the owner and have been using it for many years. It is an interesting, loosely textured bread with an unusual light-brown color and a rich, full flavor. It is delicious with sweet butter, and it keeps well.

[2 small loaves]

1 cup coarse rolled oats
1 cup boiling water
2 packages active dry yeast
1 teaspoon granulated sugar
½ cup warm water (100° to 115°, approximately)
1 cup warm milk
1 tablespoon salt
¼ cup dark brown sugar
4 to 5 cups all-purpose flour, approximately

Cook the oats in the boiling water until thickened, about 3 minutes. Pour into a large mixing bowl and allow to cool to lukewarm. Meanwhile, stir the yeast and teaspoon of sugar into the warm water until dissolved, and allow to proof. Add the warm milk, salt, brown sugar, and yeast mixture to the oats and stir well, then stir in 4 cups of flour, 1 cup at a time. Turn out on a floured board. Knead into a smooth, pliable, elastic dough, if necessary using as much as ½ to 1 cup, or more, of additional flour to get it to the right feel. (This will take about 10 minutes.) Shape the dough into a ball, put into a well-buttered bowl, and turn to coat on all sides. Cover and let rise in a warm, draft-free place until doubled in bulk, 1 to 1½ hours.

Punch the dough down. Knead for 2 or 3 minutes and shape into two loaves. Thoroughly butter two 8 x 4 x 2-inch tins. Place the dough in the tins, cover, and let rise in a warm place until about even with the top of the tins, or amost doubled in bulk.

Preheat the oven to 375°, place the bread in the center of the lowest rack, and bake for about 45 to 50 minutes, until the loaves sound hollow when tapped on top and bottom with the knuckles. Return the loaves, without the tins, to the oven rack to bake for about 5 minutes and acquire a firmer crust. Remove the loaves to a rack and cool.

NOTE
If you should want a very soft top crust, brush the loaves with melted butter when you bring them out of the oven.

SWEETENED BREADS AND COFFEE CAKES

Mother's Raisin Bread

This was a raisin bread that my mother made very often, modeled on one she had admired at the Palace Hotel in San Francisco. During World War I she used to do benefit teas for the British Red Cross, and there were always requests for this bread, thinly sliced and spread with good sweet butter. It was arranged on large platters, and there was never any of it left.

[2 loaves]

1 package active dry yeast
2 cups lukewarm milk
⅓ cup granulated sugar
1 tablespoon salt
3 tablespoons butter
5 to 6 cups all-purpose flour
Melted butter
1½ cups sultana raisins plumped overnight
   in sherry or Cognac to barely cover,
   ½ teaspoon ground mace, and 2 teaspoons
   grated fresh orange rind
1 egg yolk, beaten with 2 tablespoons cream

◀ Dissolve the yeast in ¼ cup of the warm milk and proof it. Combine the rest of the warm milk, sugar, salt, and 3 tablespoons butter in a large bowl. Add the yeast mixture, then, using one hand or a heavy wooden spoon, gradually stir in enough flour to make a stiff dough. Turn out on a floured surface and knead for about 10 minutes, until smooth, elastic, and glossy. Place in a buttered bowl and turn to coat the surface with butter. Cover and set in a warm, draft-free spot to rise until doubled in bulk, about 2½ hours.

Punch the dough down and knead for 3 minutes. Return to the bowl and let rise again for 30 minutes. Divide the dough into two equal pieces and roll each out into a rectangle about 7 x 20 inches. Brush with melted butter and sprinkle with the raisin mixture. Roll the dough up tightly;

tuck the ends under. Fit each roll, seam side down, in two well-buttered 8 x 4 x 2-inch loaf pans. Cover and let rise in a warm spot till the dough shows just above the top of the pans. Brush with the egg yolk-and-cream wash and bake in a preheated 400° oven for 10 minutes, then reduce the heat to 350° and continue baking for 20 to 30 minutes or until the loaves sound hollow when tapped on top and bottom. If necessary, return the loaves to the oven rack without their pans to brown the bottom crusts.

pinch with thumbs

Raisin and Nut Bread

This can be baked in two loaves with a mixture of raisins and nuts in both or with raisins in one loaf and nuts in the other. It is a good, all-purpose bread, which is enhanced by the extra sweetness of the honey and raisins. It toasts well; it is delicious cut thin, buttered well, and served with tea or coffee; it makes interesting sweet sandwiches when filled with chopped nuts and fruits, chopped figs, or even chopped olives and nuts; and it is also very good with marmalades of various kinds.

[2 loaves]

1 package active dry yeast
2 tablespoons honey
½ cup warm water (100° to 115°, approximately)
½ stick (¼ cup) butter, cut in small pieces
1¾ cups warm milk
5 to 6½ cups all-purpose flour
1½ to 2 teaspoons salt
½ cup raisins, or to taste (see note below)
½ cup chopped walnuts, pecans, or
    unsalted peanuts; coarsely chopped filberts;
    or almonds, or to taste
Melted butter (optional)

◄ Dissolve the yeast in the water with honey and allow to proof. Warm the butter in the milk, and add to the yeast mixture. Stir in the flour, mixed with the salt, 1 cup at a time, beating well with a wooden spoon after each addition. When the dough becomes rather stiff and difficult to stir, turn out on a floured board. Knead, adding small quantities of flour, until the dough is soft, velvety, and elastic. (It should spring back when pressed with the fingers and blister easily.) Shape the dough into a ball, place in a buttered bowl, and roll around to coat with butter on all sides. Cover tightly and let rise in a warm, draft-free place until doubled in bulk.

Punch the dough down. Turn out on a floured board and let rest for 5 minutes, then knead in the raisins and chopped nuts.

(If you are making one raisin loaf and one nut loaf, divide the dough into two equal pieces, and knead in the extra ingredients separately.) When the nuts and raisins are thoroughly amalgamated in the dough, cut it in half and shape into two loaves. Place in two well-buttered 9 x 5 x 3-inch bread pans, and allow to rise until doubled in bulk, or until the dough comes up above the tops of the pans.

Bake in a preheated 400° oven 25 to 35 minutes, or until the loaves sound hollow when tapped on the bottom with the knuckles. Remove from the tins and allow to bake on the rack in the oven for several minutes more to add color and texture to the crust. (For a tender crust brush the loaves with melted butter just as you bring them out of the oven.) Allow them to cool on racks before slicing.

NOTES

1. It is better if the raisins have soaked in a little warm water or some Cognac for an hour or so. I sometimes add a tiny bit of cinnamon or nutmeg, too, because I like these flavors with the raisins.

2. These loaves freeze well, and will keep in plastic bags in the refrigerator for several days.

Currant Bread

This bread, which I used to eat very often as a child, is a rich, flavorful, extremely pleasant loaf that keeps well and toasts magnificently. It is perfect cut very thin and spread with sweet butter and cheese, and it's a good base for sweet sandwiches like those filled with cream cheese and nuts.

[1 large loaf or 2 smaller loaves]

1 cup milk
½ cup plus 3 tablespoons granulated sugar
2½ teaspoons salt
1 stick (½ cup) plus 6 tablespoons butter
2 packages active dry yeast
1 cup lukewarm water
6 cups sifted all-purpose flour, approximately
1½ cups currants, soaked for 1 hour
 in rum, Cognac, or sherry
Melted butter

◄ Heat the milk and stir in the 3 tablespoons sugar, the salt, and the 6 tablespoons butter. Dissolve the yeast in the lukewarm water and add to the milk mixture. Stir in 3 cups sifted flour and beat until thoroughly smooth. Gradually add another 3 cups, or enough flour to make a smooth, kneadable dough. Turn the dough out on a board and knead until thoroughly blended and elastic, about 10 to 12 minutes. (If you use an electric mixer with a dough hook, knead about 5 to 6 minutes.) Put the dough in a buttered bowl and turn to coat the surface. Cover with a cloth, and set it in a warm, draft-free place to rise until doubled in bulk.

Punch the dough down, turn it out onto a board again, and knead in the ½ cup sugar, the ½ cup butter, softened, and the currants, drained and lightly floured. Form the dough into two small loaves or one long loaf and put into two buttered 8-inch pans or one 10-inch pan. Brush with melted butter and let rise in a warm place until they have increased about 60 percent. Bake in a preheated 400° oven for 50 minutes, or until the loaves are nicely browned and sound hollow when rapped top and bottom with the knuckles. Cool thoroughly on racks before slicing.

Whole-Wheat Nut Bread

The addition of toasted pine nuts and a few raisins gives this loaf its distinction, both in texture and in flavor.

[1 large loaf or 2 smaller loaves]

2 packages active dry yeast
2 tablespoons granulated sugar
1½ cups warm water (100° to 115°, approximately)
4 cups whole-wheat flour
1¾ to 2 cups all-purpose flour, or more if needed
1 tablespoon salt
¾ cup milk
½ cup honey
2 tablespoons melted butter
¼ cup pine nuts, toasted for 3 minutes
¼ cup raisins, preferably soaked in
    a little sherry or Cognac

Combine the yeast and the sugar in ½ cup of the warm water, and let proof. Combine with the flours and salt in a large mixing bowl. Make a well in the flour mixture and add the remaining cup warm water, the milk, and the honey. Blend well, adding additional all-purpose flour if the dough seems too sticky and soft to knead. Finally add the melted butter. Turn out on a floured board and knead until smooth and elastic, about 10 to 12 minutes. Place the dough in a large buttered bowl and turn to coat with butter on all sides. Cover and let rise in a warm, draft-free place until doubled in bulk.

Punch the dough down and knead in the nuts and the raisins. Divide the dough into two pieces, form into two loaves, and place in well-buttered 9 x 5 x 3-inch loaf tins, or else form one large loaf and bake in a buttered 12-inch tin. Cover and let rise again until doubled in bulk. Bake in a preheated 425° oven for 10 minutes, then reduce the heat to 350° and continue baking for 25 to 30 minutes, or until the bread sounds hollow when tapped with the knuckles. Cool on a rack.

Pistachio Bread

This is a rather sweet bread—actually, more like a coffee cake, of the type once called a "race track"—flavored with delicious, beautifully green pistachio nuts. It is rolled, formed into a very large ring, and sliced before baking. It looks and tastes extraordinarily good, and is certainly one of the best breads of this kind I have ever had. It provides about 12 servings.

[1 ring loaf]

1 package active dry yeast
Granulated sugar
¼ cup warm water (100° to 115°, approximately)
1 cup warm milk
½ stick (¼ cup) softened butter
2 teaspoons salt
3 to 4 cups all-purpose flour
¼ cup melted butter
1 cup shelled, salted pistachio nuts, coarsely chopped
1 egg, lightly beaten

❧ Combine the yeast, 1 tablespoon sugar, and water in a large mixing bowl, and allow to proof. Then add the milk, the softened butter, the salt, and ½ cup sugar to the yeast mixture. Add the flour, cup by cup, beating well after each addition. (This dough is easy to handle but will be a little sticky at this stage.) Turn out on a lightly floured board and knead for a good 10 minutes, or until smooth and elastic. Form into a ball, place in a buttered bowl, and turn to coat the surface with butter. Cover with plastic wrap and set in a warm, draft-free spot to double in bulk.

Punch the dough down and turn out on a floured board. Let rest for a few minutes, then roll into a rectangle about 18 x 12 inches. Brush the surface with the melted butter and sprinkle with ⅓ cup additional sugar and the coarsely chopped pistachio nuts. Beginning with the long edge of the rectangle, roll up the dough like a jelly roll, pressing each seam as you do so. Join the ends of the roll and pinch together to form a ring.

Place the ring carefully on a buttered baking sheet. Slice two-thirds of the way down into the ring, at ¾-inch intervals. Twist each slice to the right so that the interior of the slice is now facing upwards. Let the ring rise in a warm, draft-free place until almost doubled in size. Brush the entire surface with beaten egg, then bake in a preheated 375° oven for 30 to 35 minutes until nicely browned. Cool on a rack before serving.

Rich Sour-Cream Coffee Cake

This is another coffee bread, baked in a tube pan, one that I have enjoyed all my life. In fact, it is my favorite of all the sweet breads. The apricot glaze gives it a superb color and sheen, and the flavor makes it a rich, delicious accompaniment to coffee or tea.

[2 ring loaves]

FOR THE DOUGH:
4 packages active dry yeast
½ cup granulated sugar
½ cup warm water (100° to 115°, approximately)
1 teaspoon salt
½ cup cold milk
1 cup sour cream
2 teaspoons lemon juice
1 teaspoon vanilla extract
3 egg yolks
3 sticks (1½ cups) softened sweet butter
5 to 6 cups all-purpose flour

FOR THE FILLING:
2 tablespoons melted sweet butter
¼ cup brown or white sugar mixed with
    1 teaspoon ground cinnamon
¼ to ½ cup currants, presoaked, preferably
    in brandy, for 1 hour
¼ cup finely chopped nuts

FOR THE GLAZE:
1 one-pound jar apricot jam or preserves
    (preferably without pectin)
1 tablespoon brandy, Cointreau, or Grand Marnier

✒Combine the yeast, ¼ cup of the sugar, and lukewarm water in a large bowl, and allow to proof. Stir in the remaining ¼ cup of sugar, salt, milk, sour cream, lemon juice, and vanilla and mix well. Add the egg yolks and blend. With your fingertips, rapidly work the butter into 5 cups of the flour as you would for pie dough, to produce a dry, meal-like consistency. Add this to the yeast mixture and begin to knead in the bowl, adding more flour if necessary, to make a smooth, elastic dough. Turn out on a lightly floured board and knead 5 to 6 minutes. Shape into a ball and place in a lightly buttered bowl, turning to coat the surface with butter. Cover tightly and refrigerate to let rise for at least 4 hours or until doubled in bulk. Remove from the refrigerator, punch down, and turn out on a lightly floured board. (The dough can be kept in the refrigerator for as long as 3 days, in which case it should be punched down twice a day, until ready to roll out.)

Divide the dough in half, and roll out each piece into a rectangle about 10 x 14 inches. Brush each rectangle with melted butter, and sprinkle with the brown or white sugar and cinnamon. Over this sprinkle the

pressing down filling and rolling up.

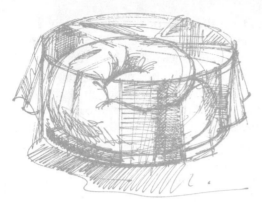

drained currants and then the finely chopped nuts. Gently press the filling into the dough with the rolling pin. Roll up from the wide end, jelly-roll fashion. Heavily butter two 9-inch tube pans. Carefully fit the rolls into the pans so that the ends of the dough join. Cover and let rise until doubled in bulk. Bake in a preheated 375° oven 45 to 55 minutes, until they are golden brown and give off a hollow sound when rapped with the knuckles. Let cool for 15 minutes in the pans, then invert on a rack. Meanwhile, melt the apricot jam over low heat. Add the brandy, Cointreau, or Grand Marnier, and blend. Strain, and coat the sides and top of the cakes with the glaze while the cakes are still warm. Cool them thoroughly before slicing.

Monkey Bread

This is a sensationally good and oddly textured sweet bread or coffee cake. It has been known as monkey bread for as long as I can remember. I have never seen an explanation for the name; perhaps it has stuck because of the bread's silly shape. I have also heard it called bubble bread. It is made in a tube pan, and if you follow directions carefully you will have a very light finished product that can be cooled and sliced or served warm and pulled apart in little clumps. You must, however, take special care in the baking to see that it is thoroughly cooked before it comes out of the oven.

[1 ring loaf]

2 packages active dry yeast
1 cup granulated sugar
½ cup warm water (100° to 115°, approximately)
2 sticks (1 cup) softened sweet butter
1½ tablespoons salt
1 cup warm milk
3 eggs, plus 2 egg yolks
6 to 7 cups all-purpose flour
½ cup brown sugar
½ cup currants, presoaked

Combine the yeast, white sugar, and water in a large mixing bowl. While this is proofing, stir 1 stick of the butter and the salt into the warm milk. (The butter does not need to melt completely.) Add to the yeast mixture. Stir in the whole eggs and egg yolks. Beat with a wooden spoon or with the hands to blend thoroughly. Add the flour, 1 cup at a time, stirring well after each addition. (After the first 5 cups it will get harder to incorporate the flour and the dough will be very sticky.) Turn out on a floured board, and using a baker's scraper or large spatula, scrape under the flour on the board, lift the dough, and fold it over. Continue this procedure, adding more flour until the dough is no longer sticky and can be kneaded with your hands. Knead a full 10 minutes, until the dough is elastic and pliable. Shape into a ball and put in a buttered bowl, turning to coat all over with butter. Cover with plastic wrap and set in a warm, draft-free place to rise until doubled in bulk. Punch the dough down and let rest for 5 minutes. Turn out on a lightly floured board (using about 1 tablespoon flour) and again shape into a ball. Let rest for another 5 to 10 minutes. Meanwhile, butter a 10-inch tube pan.

In a saucepan, melt the second stick of sweet butter with the brown sugar and currants. Pinch off enough dough to make golf ball-sized balls. Roll the balls in the butter mixture, line the bottom of the tube pan with them, and continue to arrange them in loose layers. Pour what is left of the butter mixture over the top. Cover loosely with a foil tent and let the

dough rise to the top of the tube pan. Bake in a preheated 375° oven for about an hour; it may take a minute or two more. Tap the top; it will sound hollow when the bread is ready. (If the top browns a little too much, don't worry, because this will be served inverted.) Unmold and let cool thoroughly before slicing, or serve warm and pull apart.

Moravian Coffee Cake

This is typical of the medium-sweet, yeasty coffee cakes that one finds in Pennsylvania and other parts of the country where Moravian groups have settled. It is wonderful served freshly baked, with butter and preserves. It freezes extremely well and can be split and buttered while still frozen and reheated in foil or in the microwave oven until it is piping hot. I recommend it highly.

[2 loaves]

4 to 4½ cups all-purpose flour
2 packages active dry yeast
½ cup water
½ cup granulated sugar
1 stick (½ cup) butter
½ teaspoon salt
2 eggs
½ cup mashed potatoes (prepared
  instant can be used)
½ cup brown sugar
2 teaspoons ground cinnamon
½ cup melted butter
Confectioners' sugar icing (optional)

⌁ Stir together 2 cups of the flour and the yeast. Heat the water, sugar, butter, and salt over low heat only until warm (100° to 115°), stirring to blend. Add to the flour-yeast mixture and beat until smooth, about 2 minutes on the medium speed of an electric mixer or 300 strokes by hand. Blend in the eggs and mashed potatoes, then add 1 cup flour and beat 1 minute on the medium speed of the mixer or 150 strokes by hand. Stir in more flour to make a moderately stiff dough. Turn onto a lightly floured surface and knead until smooth and satiny, about 8 to 10 minutes. Shape into a ball and place in a lightly buttered bowl, turning to butter all sides. Cover and let rise in a warm, draft-free place until doubled, about 1½ hours.

Punch the dough down, divide in half, and let rest 10 minutes. Pat or roll each portion into a square to fit into each of two buttered 9 x 5 x 3-inch pans. Mix together the brown sugar and cinnamon. Sprinkle half the sugar-cinnamon mixture over each coffee cake. Drizzle cakes with the melted butter. Let rise in a warm place until doubled in bulk, about 1 hour. Bake in a preheated 350° oven 30 to 35 minutes. Cool in pans five minutes. Remove from pans.

VARIATION

• If you like a sweeter cake, drizzle it with confectioners' sugar icing while warm.

• **Confectioners' Sugar Icing:** 1 egg white, pinch salt, 1 to 1½ cups confectioners' sugar, ½ teaspoon vanilla. Beat the egg white with the salt until it holds soft peaks. Fold in the sugar, and beat until it is smooth enough to spread. Add vanilla.

Cinnamon Bread

Most cinnamon loaves are rolled with raisins and nuts, but this one has the delicate spice flavor kneaded into it. You may adjust the amount of cinnamon to taste, but I find one tablespoon is about enough. In addition to its beautiful aroma, this loaf has a rather unusual color and a nice texture. It makes very good sandwiches, such as raisin and nut, or cream cheese and jam, and is a perfect loaf for toasting.

[2 loaves]

2 packages active dry yeast
⅓ cup granulated sugar
¾ cup warm water (100° to 115°, approximately)
1¼ cups warm milk, approximately
1½ tablespoons salt
½ stick (¼ cup) softened butter
1 tablespoon ground cinnamon
5 to 6 cups all-purpose flour

◆ Combine the yeast, sugar, and water in a large bowl and let proof for 5 minutes. Heat the milk, and add the salt and butter. Add to the yeast mixture and blend well. Stir in the cinnamon, then add up to 4½ cups flour, one cup at a time, beating well after each addition. Scrape the dough out on a lightly floured board, and knead a good 10 minutes or until smooth and elastic, using enough of the remaining flour to avoid excessive sticking. Shape into a ball and put into a buttered bowl, turning to coat the surface of the dough with butter. Cover with plastic wrap and let sit in a warm, draft-free spot until doubled in bulk.

Punch down the dough. Divide into two pieces, and shape into loaves that will fit two buttered 8 x 4 x 2 or 9 x 5 x 3-inch tins. Cover loosely and let rise again until doubled in bulk. Bake in a preheated 425° oven for 10 minutes, then lower the temperature to 350° and continue baking 20 to 25 minutes longer, or until the loaves sound hollow when rapped on top and bottom. Cool on racks before slicing.

VARIATIONS

• One or 2 eggs can be added to this dough, in which case you will have to increase the flour content.

• For a rich, golden top crust, brush with beaten egg just before baking.

Swedish Limpa

Unlike the usual recipe for limpa, which is so popular all through the Scandinavian countries, this calls for beer and extra honey, which gives it quite a distinctive quality. The dough is very pleasant to handle, and the finished bread has great flavor, nice texture, and an attractive appearance.

[1 large free-form loaf or 2 small free-form loaves]

1 package active dry yeast
1 teaspoon granulated sugar
¼ cup warm water (100° to 115°, approximately)
2 cups ale or beer heated to lukewarm
¼ to ½ cup honey
2 tablespoons melted butter
2 teaspoons salt
1 teaspoon ground cardamom (optional)
1 tablespoon caraway seeds or
    ¾ teaspoon aniseed, crushed
2 tablespoons chopped candied or fresh grated
    orange peel
2½ cups rye flour
3 cups all-purpose flour, unbleached if preferred

◄੩Dissolve the yeast and sugar in the water in a large bowl and let proof for 5 minutes. Combine the lukewarm ale or beer, the ¼ to ½ cup honey (depending on how sweet a bread you like), the butter, and salt and stir well. Add to the yeast mixture. Add the cardamom, caraway seeds, or aniseed, and the fresh or candied orange peel. Mix the rye and white flours together. Add 3 cups of this to the liquid mixture and beat very hard with a wooden spoon. Cover with a cloth or foil and let rise in a warm place for about 45 minutes to 1 hour. Stir down and add enough remaining flour to make a fairly stiff, although sticky dough. Turn out on a board, using ½ to ¾ cup additional flour if needed to work the dough until smooth and elastic. Knead well, and while the dough will not lose its tackiness entirely, it will become much smoother. Shape into a ball, place in a buttered bowl, and turn to coat with butter on all sides. Cover the dough and let rise until doubled in bulk, about 45 minutes to 1 hour. Punch down, shape into one large ball or two smaller balls, and place on a greased baking sheet. Brush with butter, cover loosely with waxed paper or plastic wrap, and refrigerate for at least 2 hours and preferably 3. Remove from the refrigerator and let sit, uncovered, at room temperature for 10 to 15 minutes. Then bake in a preheated oven at 375° until the bread sounds hollow when tapped on the bottom, which will take about 1 hour or 15 to 20 minutes more for the large loaf and 40 to 45 minutes for the small loaves. Cool on racks before slicing.

Kugelhopf

This is supposedly a recipe that Marie Antoinette took with her from Austria to France, where it became increasingly popular. It is traditionally baked in a special Kugelhopf mold, which gives it a festive look. Thus it makes a delightful holiday bread. Kugelhopf is an excellent coffee cake or breakfast bread, especially with fresh butter and honey. It can also be served topped with fruit, and it makes delicious toast indeed.

[1 Kugelhopf mold loaf]

1 package active dry yeast
½ cup granulated sugar
½ cup warm water (100° to 115°, approximately)
4 cups all-purpose flour
1 stick (½ cup) softened butter
1 tablespoon salt
6 eggs
¾ cup light raisins
½ cup sliced almonds

Dissolve the yeast with the sugar in the warm water and let it proof. Sift the flour, putting 2 cups in each of two bowls. Set one bowl aside. Work together 2 cups of flour and the soft butter (this may be done in the electric mixer). Mix in the salt and the eggs, one at a time, beating until very thoroughly incorporated. In alternate batches, add the remaining 2 cups flour and the yeast mixture. Mix in the electric mixer or with a wooden spoon until thoroughly blended and elastic, then stir in the raisins. Put in a large, lightly floured bowl, cover with a towel, and let rise in a warm, draft-free spot until doubled in bulk, about 1 to 1½ hours.

Punch the dough down. Heavily butter a standard 10-inch Kugelhopf mold or a 10-inch tube pan and sprinkle half the sliced almonds around the bottom of the mold (the butter will make them adhere). Pour or spoon half the dough into the mold, sprinkle in the rest of the almonds, and add the remaining dough. Let rise again until doubled in bulk, about 1 hour. Bake in a preheated oven at 475° for 10 minutes, then reduce the heat to 350° and continue baking until nicely browned,

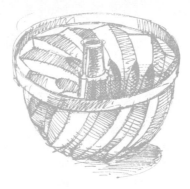

about 40 to 45 minutes. Remove from the oven and let stand for 3 minutes in the pan, then invert onto a cooling rack.

Doris Licht's ceramic Kugelhopf mold

Verterkake

A very special Norwegian sweet bread baked in round loaves, *verterkake* takes its name from *verterol*, or brewer's wort, one of the ingredients, which is a nonalcoholic beer very popular in Norway. *Verterol* used to be imported into this country, but since it is no longer available, dark beer can be substituted in its place. The bread is densely textured and has a highly interesting, spicy flavor, but I will tell you at the outset that the dough is difficult to work with. Therefore it is best to prepare it for the special occasions when you want a showoff loaf. It keeps extremely well, and is different enough from run-of-the-mill bread to warrant your mastering it. Serve it thinly sliced and well buttered, along with marmalade or jam.

The recipe comes from the Norwegian Government School for Domestic Science Teachers.

[2 free-form loaves]

2 packages active dry yeast
1¼ cups lukewarm milk
4 cups all-purpose flour
4 cups rye flour
⅔ cup lukewarm golden syrup or corn syrup
1¾ cups verterol (brewer's wort) or dark beer
¾ teaspoon ground cloves
¾ teaspoon freshly ground pepper
1 tablespoon salt
½ cup granulated sugar
½ cup raisins

◆ Proof the yeast in the lukewarm milk. Add 2 cups flour and stir to make a soft dough. Put in a warm place for 35 to 40 minutes, until the dough has started to ferment and shows some signs of rising. At this point add the lukewarm syrup and the *verterol* or beer, which has been mixed with the spices, salt, and sugar. Add the remaining flour, 1 cup at a time, until the dough becomes supple, but just firm enough to hold its shape. (This step is crucial, because too firm a dough will not rise well, and too soft a dough cannot be formed into stable loaves.) Cover and place in a warm, draft-free spot and let rise until doubled in bulk.

Punch the dough down, turn out on a floured board, fold in the raisins, and knead for a few moments. Then form into two round loaves. Place on a buttered and floured baking sheet, cover, and let rise until about doubled in bulk. Brush with hot water and prick rather lightly. Bake in a preheated 375° oven for about 45 minutes, until the crusts have become quite shiny (because of the syrup) and the loaves sound hollow when rapped on the top and bottom. Cool thoroughly before slicing, and keep refrigerated until ready to use.

NOTE

If the loaves are brushed with a thin paste made with about 2 tablespoons potato flour and a little water, just before they are taken out of the oven, they will acquire a fine, even shinier crust.

VARIATION

• For an interesting variation, use finely cut oatmeal for a third of the all-purpose and rye flours in the recipe.

EGG BREADS

Challah   Water-Proofed
Portuguese Sweet   Water-Proofed Egg Twists
Italian Holiday   Brioche
County Fair

Challah

This traditional Jewish bread has lightness and a nice color. The loaves are formed with either three or six braids, glazed with egg, and sprinkled with poppy seeds. They emerge from the oven a rich golden brown attractively flecked with the seeds. Challah is not a sweet bread but a delicate, well-textured egg bread of some richness.

[2 braided loaves]

3 packages active dry yeast
1⅓ cups warm water (100° to 115°, approximately)
1 tablespoon granulated sugar
1 tablespoon coarse salt
3 tablespoons softened butter
3 eggs
5 to 5½ cups all-purpose flour
1 egg yolk mixed with 1 teaspoon cold water
Poppy seeds

◄ Proof the yeast in the lukewarm water in a large bowl. Add the sugar, salt, butter, eggs, and 5 cups of the flour, a cup at a time. Beat thoroughly with a wooden spoon or with the hands. Gradually add more flour until the dough is very stiff. Turn the dough out on a board sprinkled with flour. Knead until the dough is smooth and elastic, approximately 10 minutes.

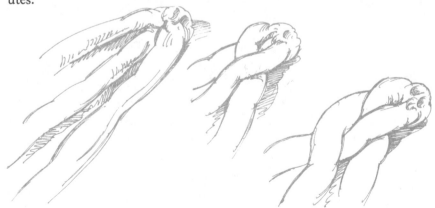

Place the dough in a very large buttered bowl, and turn to coat the surface with butter. Cover and let rise in a warm, draft-free place until doubled in bulk, about 1½ to 2 hours. Punch the dough down and divide into six equal parts. Roll each portion into a rope about 1 inch in diameter on a lightly floured board. Braid three ropes together to make two loaves. Place the breads about 6 inches apart on a buttered baking sheet. Cover and let rise in a warm place until almost doubled in bulk. Brush the tops of the loaves with the egg wash and sprinkle with poppy seeds. Bake in a preheated 400° oven for 35 to 45 minutes, or until the loaves sound hollow when tapped with the knuckles. Cool on racks.

Portuguese Sweet Bread

Anyone who has spent time on Cape Cod or Nantucket remembers the delicious light, round loaves of Portuguese bread found there, which resembles the egg bread of other countries. This recipe makes a delicate, spongy bread that is a delight. It has a fine crumb and is excellent for breakfast or tea. It demands the addition of good sweet butter and marmalade, honey, or jam.

[2 round loaves]

2 packages active dry yeast
1 cup plus 1 teaspoon granulated sugar
½ cup lukewarm water
1 stick (½ cup) softened butter
½ cup warm milk
4 eggs, lightly beaten
1 tablespoon salt
4 to 4½ cups all-purpose flour, approximately

Combine the yeast, 1 teaspoon sugar, and water in a large bowl and allow to proof. Put the butter in the warm milk, add the 1 cup sugar, and blend well. Add to the yeast mixture and stir to combine the ingredients. Add 3 of the eggs, lightly beaten, and salt and mix well. Then add 4 cups of flour, 1 cup at a time, kneading with your hands in the bowl, to make a soft dough. Turn out on a floured board and knead until the dough is smooth and elastic, using only enough additional flour to prevent sticking. This should take about 10 minutes. Shape into a ball and put in a buttered bowl, turning the dough to coat the surface with butter. Cover with plastic wrap and let rise in a warm, draft-free place until doubled in bulk.

Punch down the dough and divide into two equal pieces. Shape again into balls and place in two buttered skillets—ones that can be used in the oven and that measure about 9 inches in diameter at the top. (Teflon works perfectly for this, but plain omelet skillets will do nicely.) Or you may use two 8½ x 4½ x 2½ bread pans. Cover loosely and let rise again until doubled in bulk. Brush the tops with the remaining egg, well beaten, and bake in a preheated oven at 350° for about 30 minutes, or until the bread is a rich, dark, shining color and sounds hollow when rapped on top and bottom. Cool on racks before slicing.

Italian Holiday Bread

This is a rather sweet brioche-type bread, exceedingly light and baked free form. It is a pleasant bread for tea or breakfast, toasts extremely well, and can be used for certain types of sandwiches, such as candied ginger and cream cheese or orange marmalade and walnut. It can also be made as a braided loaf, or baked in a fanciful form; for instance, you could use a flowerpot (well buttered with a piece of aluminum foil on the bottom to cover the hole), clustering three little topknots of dough on top.

[2 free-form loaves]

Judith's flowerpot bread

2 packages active dry yeast
Brown sugar
½ cup warm water (100° to 115°, approximately)
½ cup melted butter
2 whole eggs plus 3 egg yolks
1 teaspoon salt
4 to 4½ cups all-purpose flour
1 egg yolk combined with 2 teaspoons flour,
    2 teaspoons sugar, and 2 teaspoons water

Dissolve the yeast and ½ cup brown sugar in warm water in a mixing bowl and allow to proof. Stir in the melted butter, whole eggs, egg yolks, and salt and blend well. Add the flour, 1 cup at a time, beating it in with a wooden spoon or with the hand. Turn the dough out on a floured board, and knead with additional flour until you have a soft, velvety, elastic dough with no trace of stickiness. (A good 5 minutes of concentrated kneading should accomplish this.)

Divide the dough into two equal portions. Flatten and shape each into a round loaf. Place on a greased baking sheet, cover with a tent of aluminum foil, and let rise in a warm, draft-free place until doubled in bulk, 1 to 2 hours. Brush the egg mixture over the tops of the two loaves and slash once or twice with a sharp knife or razor blade. Sprinkle with additional sugar, if desired, and bake in a preheated 325° oven 35 to 40 minutes, or until the bread sounds hollow when tapped on top and bottom with the knuckles. Cool on a rack before slicing.

Water-Proofed Bread

Although the dough in this recipe is fairly difficult to handle, it makes a very delicate, briochelike bread with a rich, buttery, eggy taste. It is extraordinarily good, ideal for tea or for eating with butter, jam, and marmalade, and toasts extremely well. It can be wrapped in plastic and frozen for 3 or 4 weeks. The bread is called "water-proofed" because the dough is submerged in a bath of water for the first rising.

[2 loaves]

2 packages active dry yeast
½ cup warm water (100° to 115°, approximately)
¼ cup plus 1 teaspoon granulated sugar
½ cup warm milk
1 stick (½ cup) butter
2 teaspoons salt
3 eggs
3½ cups all-purpose flour

◆ Rinse a 4-quart mixing bowl with warm water. Dry thoroughly. Put in the yeast, the ½ cup warm water, and the teaspoon of sugar, and stir until the yeast dissolves. Allow it to proof for 5 minutes. Heat the milk with the butter and ¼ cup sugar until lukewarm, then add to the yeast mixture. Add the salt and stir to blend well. Add the eggs, one at a time, and again blend thoroughly. Then stir in 3 cups of the flour, 1 cup at a time, to make what will probably be a very wet and sticky dough. Stir quite vigorously. Spread out the dough on a working surface—a table, a piece of marble, or a board—sprinkled with the additional ½ cup flour. Use a baker's scraper or large spatula to work in this last portion of flour and make the dough firmer. Scrape under the flour and the dough, lifting and folding inward. Repeat until the flour is well incorporated.

When the dough is easy to handle, begin kneading by hand. Continue until the dough can be shaped. (The process of kneading first with the scraper and then by hand is very effective for delicate dough. In this case the dough will remain rather sticky, but don't worry about it.)

Lift the dough, pat with
flour, and place on a clean
kitchen towel also sprinkled
with flour. Wrap it and tie it in
the towel, just as you would a
package, but very loosely.
Submerge this in a large bowl
filled with warm water (about
100° to 115°). It will sink.
Let it sit for about 35 to 40
minutes, or until it rises
sufficiently to float on top
of the water.

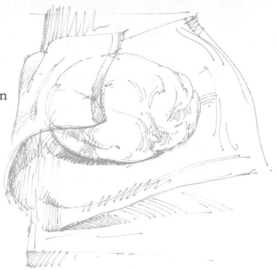

Lift the dough from the water and let the excess water drip off. Unwrap and turn out on a lightly floured surface. Again it will be quite
sticky, so scrape off any dough that adheres to the towel. Knead and shape
into two loaves, using both dough scraper and your hands. Thoroughly
butter two 9 x 5 x 3-inch pans and place one loaf in each pan. Cover,
put in a warm, draft-free place, and let the dough rise slightly above the
tops of the pans, or until almost doubled in bulk.

Meanwhile, preheat the oven to 375°. Brush the dough with cold
water, and, if you like, make a slash in each loaf with a sharp knife. Place

on the middle rack of the oven and bake for about 30 to 35 minutes, or until the loaves sound hollow when rapped with the knuckles, top and bottom. When done, place the loaves directly on the oven rack, without their pans, to brown the bottoms a little more and crisp the crusts. Cool on racks.

VARIATION

• **Salt-Free Water-Proofed Bread:** This uses the same technique as the previous recipe, except that I tailored it for someone on a special diet by leaving out the salt and substituting honey for the sugar. The honey, in turn, made a stickier dough that required an extra cup of flour. Although a little closer grained in texture than the first loaf, it is still a very delicious bread.

[2 loaves]

2 packages active dry yeast
½ cup warm water (100° to 115°, approximately)
¼ cup plus 1 tablespoon honey
½ cup milk
1 stick (½ cup) butter
3 eggs
4 to 4¼ cups all-purpose flour

Rinse out a large mixing bowl with warm water and dry it. Combine the yeast with the warm water and 1 tablespoon honey in the mixing bowl. Stir well until it is dissolved and allow to proof for 5 minutes. Heat the milk to lukewarm with the butter and remaining ¼ cup honey. Pour it into the yeast mixture and stir to blend very well. When it has cooled slightly add the eggs, one at a time. Then stir in 3½ cups of the flour, a cup at a time, with a wooden spoon. The dough will be quite sticky and wet. Sprinkle the additional ½ to ¾ cup flour on your working surface, and use a baker's scraper or large spatula and your hand to incorporate the flour into the very soft dough. Proceed as described in the master recipe, page 142.

Water-Proofed Egg Twists

These are delicious little sweet buns that lend themselves to many variations. They are fun to prepare, have extraordinary taste, look charming, and can be frozen and reheated with great success. They are very nice for breakfast or with luncheon dishes.

[About 18 buns]

1 package active dry yeast
½ cup plus 1 tablespoon granulated sugar
½ cup warm water (100° to 115°, approximately)
3½ cups all-purpose flour, or more as needed
1 teaspoon salt
1 stick (½ cup) butter, cut in pieces
¼ cup warm milk
3 eggs, lightly beaten
1 teaspoon vanilla extract
½ cup chopped walnuts, filberts, or pecans

◄¿ Proof the yeast with 1 tablespoon sugar in the warm water. Put 2 cups flour in a large mixing bowl and add the salt and butter. Rub the butter into the flour with your fingertips, working very quickly to keep the butter from melting, until the mixture resembles rather coarse meal. Add the warm milk and the yeast mixture, and beat very well with a wooden spoon. Then add the eggs, vanilla, and one more cup of flour and beat until the batter is very springy and airy. Turn out on a lightly floured board and knead for just 1 minute, until you can form the dough into a ball. Spread out a cotton or linen cloth—a kitchen tea towel is perfect —and put the dough in the center. Fold the towel over the dough as you would to wrap a package, keeping it rather loose. Secure the package with string, then submerge in a large bowl or crock of tepid water and let stand for about 35 to 40 minutes. The package will rise to the top and float. Remove and let the excess water drip off.

Unwrap the dough, which will have doubled in volume. Scrape off onto a lightly floured board, and shape into a ball, kneading in a little flour, since the dough will be fairly wet and sticky at this point. Pinch off from this ball of dough 18 or so even pieces about the size of a large egg, weighing the pieces to achieve uniformity if you have a scale and want to be a perfectionist. On a baking sheet or in a jelly-roll pan mix the ½ cup sugar and the chopped nuts. Roll each ball of dough in the sugar-and-nut

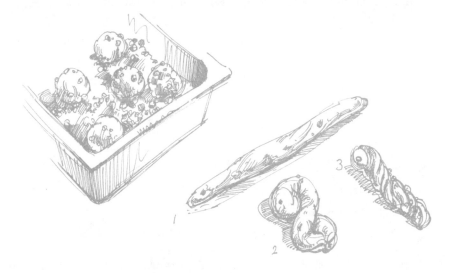

mixture into a cylinder about 7 or 8 inches long. Fasten the ends together, and then twist at the center to roughly form a figure eight. Place on well-buttered baking sheets about 2 inches apart. Cover with aluminum foil and let rise in a warm, draft-free spot for 30 to 40 minutes, until the twists are doubled in bulk. Bake in a preheated 375° oven 15 to 20 minutes, until golden in color and fairly hollow sounding when tapped on the bottom. Cool on racks.

VARIATION

• After the risen dough has been scraped onto the floured board, gently knead in the nuts. Proceed with the recipe, rolling out the pieces of dough in sugar only.

Brioche Bread

Not the classic brioche that one prepares for the little top-knotted rolls, although similar to it, this is a loaf that is especially good for delicate sandwiches, such as the popular onion sandwich hors d'oeuvre I created years ago. It is also a delicious egg bread by itself, easy to make and pleasant in flavor.

[2 loaves]

1½ packages active dry yeast
2 tablespoons granulated sugar
½ cup warm water (100° to 115°, approximately)
1 cup melted butter
1½ teaspoons salt
4 cups all-purpose flour
4 eggs
1 egg yolk mixed with ¼ cup
  evaporated milk or light cream

◆ᴢ Combine the yeast, sugar, and warm water and allow to proof. Mix the melted butter and salt. In a large bowl combine the flour, eggs, melted butter, and yeast mixture. Beat with the hand until smooth. Place in a buttered bowl, turning to butter the surface, cover, and set in a warm, draft-free place to rise until light and doubled in bulk, about 1 to 1½ hours. Punch the dough down and shape into two loaves. Fit into buttered 8 x 4 x 2-inch loaf pans and let rise again in a warm place until doubled in bulk, about 1 hour. Brush the loaves with the egg yolk-milk wash. Bake at 400° for 30 minutes, until the loaves are a deep golden brown and sound hollow when tapped with the knuckles. Cool on a rack.

County Fair Bread

When well made, this slightly sweet braided loaf looks exactly as if it would win first prize at the fair. It can be made with unbleached hard-wheat flour as well as with all-purpose flour, and the baking sheet can be coated with cornmeal instead of butter. The flavor is good, and the texture is very light. This is a nice bread to give away for a holiday present.

[1 large braided loaf or 2 smaller braided loaves]

5 to 5½ cups all-purpose or
    unbleached hard-wheat flour
¼ cup granulated sugar
2 teaspoons salt
1 package active dry yeast
1½ cups milk
½ stick (¼ cup) butter, cut in small pieces
2 eggs
1 egg white, lightly beaten with
    1 tablespoon water
Sesame seeds

◄⋜ In a large mixing bowl combine 1 cup of the flour, the sugar, salt, and dry yeast. Heat the milk and the butter in a saucepan, just until the milk is warm; the butter does not need to melt. Add the eggs and the warm milk mixture to the flour mixture. (This, as you will notice, is one of those newish dry-mix processes where you do not proof the yeast first—and it works.) Mix very well until thoroughly moistened, and beat with a wooden spoon for about 5 minutes. Then stir in the remaining flour to form a stiff dough. Turn out on a floured board, and knead the dough until it is quite smooth and elastic, about 5 minutes. Work into a ball, place in a buttered bowl, and turn to coat with butter on all sides. Cover and let rise in a warm, draft-free place until light and doubled in bulk, 1 to 1½ hours.

Punch the dough down and divide into six equal portions. Roll each of these portions into a thin cylinder about 8 to 10 inches long. Take three strips and braid them together. Place the braid on a baking sheet buttered or sprinkled with cornmeal. Braid the remaining three strips and place about 6 inches away from the other loaf. (For a more spectacular loaf, make a braid of three large strips and then a braid of three smaller strips, and put one on top of the other. This takes a good hour to bake and a slight amount of dexterity to shape.)

Cover the loaves and let rise in a warm, draft-free space until doubled in bulk, which will take another 1½ hours. Brush with the egg white and water, sprinkle lavishly with sesame seeds, and bake in a preheated 375° oven for 35 to 40 minutes, or until the loaves sound hollow when tapped top and bottom with the knuckles and have achieved a nice golden-brown color.

BATTER BREADS

Sally Lunn   Dill-Seed
Golden Cake Batter   English Muffin
English Muffin for Microwave Oven

Sally Lunn

This is an old, old recipe for Sally Lunn. I like to bake it in a large tube pan and invert it. It makes a beautiful standing loaf that, when fresh, should be torn apart with forks rather than cut, to retain its lightness. Or, after cooling, it can be sliced and toasted. If you have some left, I recommend that you freeze it and use it sliced and toasted.

[1 ring loaf]

1 package active dry yeast
⅓ cup sugar
½ cup warm water (100° to 115°, approximately)
½ cup lukewarm milk
1 stick butter, melted in the milk
1 teaspoon salt
3 eggs
3½ to 4 cups all-purpose flour

◆ Combine the yeast, sugar, and warm water in a mixing bowl, and allow to proof. Add the milk, butter, and salt, and stir well to combine. Add the eggs and incorporate them well with a wooden spoon. Then add the flour in small amounts, and beat well with a wooden spoon after each addition. Make a stiff but workable batter, using up to four cups of flour if necessary. Cover the bowl, and let the batter rise slowly in a rather cool

spot until doubled in bulk. Beat it down with a wooden spoon for about 1 minute. Scrape into a well-buttered 9- or 10-inch tube pan, and again let the batter rise—this time to the very top of the pan.

Bake in a preheated 375° oven 45 to 50 minutes or until the bread is dark and golden on top and sounds hollow when rapped with your knuckles. Turn out on a rack to cool, or serve warm, if you prefer, with sweet butter.

Golden Cake Batter Bread

A light, rather sweetish, easy-to-make bread that is similar to Sally Lunn. It will slice nicely if baked in a tube pan according to the directions, and it can be reheated, wrapped in foil and buttered if you wish, in a 350° oven for 10 to 15 minutes or in the microwave oven for 20 seconds. It makes an attractive loaf of bread for a gift.

[1 ring loaf]

4 to 4½ cups all-purpose flour
½ cup granulated sugar
1 teaspoon salt
1 package active dry yeast
1 cup milk
1 stick (½ cup) butter
2 eggs
2 teaspoons vanilla extract

◄∂ In a large bowl, combine 2 cups of flour, the sugar, salt, and yeast. Heat the milk and butter in a saucepan until the milk is warm; the butter does not need to melt. Combine with the eggs, vanilla, and the flour mixture, using an electric mixer at lowest speed until the flour is moistened; then beat 2 minutes at medium speed. By hand, stir in the remaining flour to form a stiff batter. Cover and let rise in a warm, draft-free place until doubled in bulk, about 1 hour.

Stir down the dough. Spread in a well-buttered 10-inch tube pan, then cover and let rise in a warm place until doubled in bulk, about 45 minutes. Bake in a preheated oven at 350° for 40 to 45 minutes, until golden brown. Cool for 5 minutes before removing from the pan.

Dill-Seed Bread

This is almost a batter bread. It has a nice crumb, lightness, a delicious "nose," and a very pleasant "dilly" flavor. I prefer using 2 teaspoons dill weed to the dill seed, but that is a matter of personal taste. It is not a good keeper.

[1 loaf]

1 package active dry yeast
2 teaspoons granulated sugar
¼ cup warm water (100° to 115°, approximately)
8 ounces large-curd cottage cheese
   (not the creamed type), at room temperature
1 egg, at room temperature
2 teaspoons grated onion
2 tablespoons melted butter
2 teaspoons salt
¼ teaspoon baking soda
1 cup whole-wheat flour
1½ cups all-purpose flour
2 teaspoons dill seed or dill weed

Dissolve the yeast and sugar in the warm water in a large mixing bowl, and allow to proof for about 5 minutes. Stir the cottage cheese into the yeast mixture, then add the egg and blend thoroughly. Put in the grated onion, melted butter, salt, and baking soda. Stir in the flours, 1 cup at a time, and the dill seed and turn out on a lightly floured board. Knead for about 5 minutes, or until the dough is smooth and springs back when indented with the fingers. Butter a 9 x 5 x 3-inch loaf tin and shape the dough to fit the pan. Cover and let rise in a warm, draft-free spot until doubled in bulk.

Bake in a preheated 375° oven for 35 to 40 minutes, or until the bread sounds hollow when you remove it from the pan and tap it with your knuckles. Cool on a rack before slicing.

English Muffin Bread

As its name suggests, this bread is derived from English muffin batter. Large-grained, with a fairly coarse crumb, it is excellent when sliced and toasted, otherwise, it is rather uninteresting. It may be baked in one large tin, which gives deep slices, or in two small ones.

[1 large loaf or 2 smaller loaves]

1 package active dry yeast
1 tablespoon granulated sugar
½ cup warm water (100° to 115°, approximately)
2½ cups all-purpose flour
2 teaspoons salt
⅞ cup warm milk
¼ teaspoon baking soda dissolved in
    1 tablespoon warm water

Combine the yeast, sugar, and warm water in a large bowl, stir until the yeast and sugar are dissolved, and let the mixture sit until it proofs. Add the flour, mixed with the salt, and the warm milk in alternate portions while stirring vigorously with a wooden spoon. Holding the bowl tightly, beat the dough very hard until it shows some elasticity and looks almost ready to leave the sides of the bowl. (Unlike a kneaded dough, however, it will remain loose and sticky.) When it has an almost gummy quality, cover and let rise in a warm place for about 1¼ to 1½ hours, until doubled in bulk. Stir down with a wooden spoon, add the dissolved soda, and beat vigorously again for about 1 minute, being careful to distribute the soda thoroughly, or else the bread will be streaked. Then butter one 10-inch or two 8 x 4 x 2-inch tins and fill with the dough, using a rubber spatula to scrape it from the bowl.

Let rise again in a warm place for about 1 to 1¼ hours. Bake the bread in a preheated 375° oven until it is golden on top and shrinks slightly from the sides of the pan. Cool in the pans for about 5 minutes, then turn out onto a rack. (If necessary, loosen from edges of the pans with a knife.) Cut in slices about ½ inch thick for toasting, and butter them well.

English Muffin Bread for Microwave Oven

This recipe was developed for use in a microwave oven. It will not brown during baking, but it makes wonderful toast with excellent flavor, and you don't need a brown loaf to make toast, really. This is as close to original English muffins as you can possibly get, and I find it highly satisfactory. You are going to be amused watching this bread rise in the microwave oven.

[2 loaves]

5 cups all-purpose flour, approximately
2 packages active dry yeast
1 tablespoon granulated sugar
2 teaspoons salt
2½ cups milk
¼ teaspoon baking soda dissolved in
   1 tablespoon warm water

◅ In a large mixing bowl combine 3 cups of the flour, the yeast, sugar, and salt. Heat the milk in a saucepan until warm (100° to 115°) and add to the flour mixture, beating by hand or in a mixer until quite smooth. Stir in enough of the remaining flour to make a stiff batter, adding a little more flour if needed. Cover the bowl, place in a warm place, and let the batter rise until light and doubled in bulk, about 1 hour.

Stir down the yeast batter and thoroughly blend in the dissolved soda. Divide the batter between two oiled 8½ x 4½ x 2½-inch tins or 1½ quart soufflé dishes. Cover and let rise in a warm place until doubled in bulk, about 45 minutes. Cook each loaf, uncovered, in the microwave oven for 6 minutes and 30 seconds, or until no doughy spots remain. Cool for 5 minutes, then loosen the edges and remove from the pan. Cool completely. To serve, slice and toast.

BAKING POWDER
AND
SODA BREADS

Baking Powder Biscuits

Certainly no bread in America has been more popular over a longer time than baking powder biscuits. In fact, in many homes they were baked three times a day in great quantities, and were eaten hot, with butter and honey or preserves, along with every meal. Nowadays ready-to-bake biscuits that come packaged in tubes have taken the place of the homemade. I myself have seen people buying as many as two and three dozen tubes at a time. But few commercial brands are as good as a well-made biscuit, which should be made quickly and handled as little as possible. This is the standard recipe.

[About 12 biscuits]

> 2 cups sifted all-purpose flour
> 1 tablespoon double-acting baking powder
> ½ teaspoon salt
> ½ stick (¼ cup) butter or other shortening
> ¾ cup milk

◄ Sift the flour into a mixing bowl with the baking powder and salt. Then, using your fingers or two knives (I use a heavy fork) blend the butter and flour into very fine particles. Add the milk and stir into the dough just enough to make the particles cling together. (It should be a very, very soft dough.) Turn out on a floured surface and knead for about 1 minute, then either pat or roll out.

(If you want very high, fluffy biscuits, the dough should be ½ to ¾ of an inch thick, and if you want thin, crusty biscuits, make it about ¼ inch thick.) Cut in rounds or in squares. For crisp biscuits, place far apart on an ungreased cookie sheet; for fluffier biscuits, place close together on an ungreased cookie sheet. Bake in a preheated 450° oven for about 12 to 15 minutes, and serve piping hot.

VARIATIONS
• Add chopped herbs or grated cheese to the biscuit dough.
• For drop biscuits, add another ¼ cup of milk, drop by spoonfuls onto a buttered baking sheet, and bake the same way.

Cream Biscuits

We had a reputation at home for very special biscuits, which were made by our Chinese cook, who was with us for many years. After he left us they became a standard item in our household, and I still make them very often. The secret of their unique quality is this: They use heavy cream instead of butter or shortening.

[About 12 biscuits]

2 cups all-purpose flour
1 teaspoon salt
1 tablespoon double-acting baking powder
2 teaspoons granulated sugar
¾ to 1 cup heavy cream
Melted butter

◀? Sift the dry ingredients together and fold in the heavy cream until it makes a soft dough that can be easily handled. Turn out on a floured board, knead for about 1 minute, and then pat to a thickness of about ½ to ¾ inch. Cut in rounds or squares, dip in melted butter, and arrange on a buttered baking sheet or in a square baking pan. Bake in a preheated 425° oven for 15 to 18 minutes and serve very hot.

Gingerbread

Many people consider gingerbread to be a cake, but it was originally meant to be a bread served at lunch or dinner with sweet butter. It is best, I think, served slightly warm with plenty of butter; if cold, cut it thin and spread with softened butter. The variation with chopped candied ginger gives it a surprisingly different look.

[6 good servings]

1 cup light or dark molasses
½ cup boiling water
5 tablespoons butter
½ teaspoon salt
1½ to 2 teaspoons ground ginger
1 teaspoon baking soda
2 cups all-purpose flour

Put the molasses in a mixing bowl, add the boiling water and butter, and stir until well mixed. Add the salt, ginger, and soda and stir lightly. Then stir in just enough flour to moisten and mix the ingredients. Turn into a 9 x 9 x 2-inch baking pan. Bake at 375° for 25 to 35 minutes, or until the top springs back when pressed lightly and the bread pulls away from the sides of the pan.

VARIATION
• Sprinkle chopped candied ginger on top of the bread before baking, which will give it a very dark, flecked outer appearance. The baking time may be a few minutes longer.

Irish Whole-Wheat Soda Bread

Traditionally, soda bread is baked over a peat fire in a three-legged iron pot that can be raised or lowered over the fire in the old-fashioned way. Soda bread is very different from any other bread you can find in the world. It's round, with a cross cut in the top, and it has a velvety texture, quite unlike yeast bread, and the most distinctive and delicious taste. Sliced paper thin and buttered, it is one of the best tea or breakfast breads I know, and it makes wonderful toast for any meal.

[1 round loaf]

3 cups whole-wheat flour
1 cup all-purpose flour
1 tablespoon kosher salt or 2 teaspoons regular salt
1 level teaspoon baking soda
¾ teaspoon double-acting baking powder
1½ to 2 cups buttermilk

◄ Combine the dry ingredients and mix thoroughly to distribute the soda and baking powder, then add enough buttermilk to make a soft dough, similar in quality to biscuit dough but firm enough to hold its shape. Knead on a lightly floured board for 2 or 3 minutes, until quite smooth and velvety. Form into a round loaf and place in a well-buttered 8-inch cake pan or on a well-buttered cookie sheet. Cut a cross on the top of the loaf with a very sharp, floured knife. Bake in a preheated 375° oven for 35 to 40 minutes, or until the loaf is nicely browned and sounds

hollow when rapped with the knuckles. (The cross will have spread open, which is characteristic of soda bread.) Let the loaf cool before slicing very thin; soda bread must never be cut thick.

VARIATION
• For white soda bread, use 4 cups all-purpose flour, preferably un-bleached, and the same amounts of salt and baking powder called for in the master recipe, but decrease the baking soda to ¾ teaspoon. Otherwise, the bread is prepared in exactly the same way as in the master recipe.

Helen Evans Brown's Corn Chili Bread

The late Helen Evans Brown was a specialist in California's traditional foods. This recipe of hers is an extremely moist, rich bread that is delicious with plenty of butter. It can be served with such things as roast pork or a roast turkey or even with a good stew. It is one of my oldest bread recipes, and one of my very favorites. As a matter of fact, I have often served it for large parties, doubling the recipe, which is very simple.

[9 to 10 servings]

3 ears of fresh, uncooked corn
1 cup yellow cornmeal
2 teaspoons salt
3 teaspoons double-acting baking powder
1 cup sour cream
¾ cup melted butter
2 eggs, well beaten
¼ pound Gruyère or Monterey Jack cheese, very finely diced
1 4-ounce can peeled green chilis, finely chopped

◆ Scrape the kernels from the corn cobs and combine with the remaining ingredients. Pour into a well-buttered 9-inch-square baking dish or 2½-quart soufflé dish. Bake in a preheated 350° oven for 1 hour. Serve with melted butter or with the sauce from the main dish.

Clay's Cornsticks

Cornsticks are different in their way from cornbread. They are baked in a mold shaped like a row of corn ears. The mold is heated as hot as possible after you have greased it with bacon fat, goose grease, or homemade lard, which will give a good flavor and won't burn the way butter will. The cornsticks usually bake to a golden color and are puffy inside and deliciously crunchy on the outside. For a variation, add 2 tablespoons of fresh grated corn.

This recipe will make about 14 sticks. Most cornstick molds make 7 or 8, so you can bake one batch, quickly regrease the mold, and bake another batch during the meal. Before using a new mold it is wise to follow the rules for curing it, generally given on the label. Then try these very good, simple-to-make cornsticks.

"Clay" is Clayton Triplette, who has been my assistant and housekeeper for many years, and who is no mean cook himself.

[About 14 cornsticks]

1 cup all-purpose flour
1 cup cornmeal, preferably stone ground
   if you can get it
3 teaspoons double-acting baking powder
½ teaspoon salt
1 cup milk or buttermilk
2 tablespoons melted butter
2 eggs

◄꜆ Sift the dry ingredients together, and stir in the milk and melted butter to make a light batter, along with the eggs. Generously grease the mold with any fat except butter and heat until very hot. Spoon the batter into the mold to make it three-quarters full. Bake in a preheated 400° oven 18 to 20 minutes, until the cornsticks are brown and puffy. Remove at once, regrease the mold, and refill with the remaining batter. Serve the cornsticks hot from the molds with plenty of butter.

Boston Brown Bread

This is as American as any food can be because it was created by our early settlers as an accompaniment for Boston baked beans. It has a delicious personality of its own. I remember that in our house it was steamed in baking powder tins, which produced a lovely cylindrical loaf, after which it was dried out for a short time in the oven. The one-pound baking powder tins we used to get are no longer quite the same. Nowadays you might try one-pound coffee cans, although they are larger. This recipe will make enough for 2 one-pound tins or 4 half-pound baking powder tins.

1 cup rye meal
1 cup cornmeal
1 cup graham flour
¾ tablespoon baking soda
2 teaspoons salt
¾ cup molasses
2 cups buttermilk

⊸ Combine the dry ingredients, add the molasses and the buttermilk, and stir until very well mixed. Then pour two-thirds full into well-buttered 1-pound molds—1-pound coffee tins or baking tins or any type of mold that will be airtight; the long tins in which English biscuits come are ideal, too. (Be sure to butter the lid as well as the tin.) Cover the lid with foil and tie it so it will be watertight. Place the mold on a trivet or a rack in a large kettle containing enough boiling water to come halfway up around the mold. Cover the kettle tightly and steam for 1½ to 2 hours, adding more boiling water if needed. Remove the bread and dry slightly in a 350° oven. Eat warm, with plenty of butter.

VARIATION
• Add 1 cup raisins to the dough before steaming.

Carl Gohs' Zucchini Bread

This rather unusual loaf has a very pleasant flavor, a little on the sweet side, and a distinctive texture. The built-in moisture provided by the zucchini makes it a very good keeper. It can be prepared with 1 cup of whole-wheat flour instead of all white flour.

[2 loaves]

3 eggs
2 cups granulated sugar
1 cup vegetable oil
2 cups grated, peeled raw zucchini
3 teaspoons vanilla extract
3 cups all-purpose flour
1 teaspoon salt
1 teaspoon baking soda
¼ teaspoon double-acting baking powder
3 teaspoons ground cinnamon
1 cup coarsely chopped filberts or walnuts

◄ Beat the eggs until light and foamy. Add the sugar, oil, zucchini, and vanilla and mix lightly but well. Combine the flour, salt, soda, baking powder, and cinnamon and add to the egg-zucchini mixture. Stir until well blended, add nuts, and pour into two 9 x 5 x 3-inch greased loaf pans. Bake in a preheated 350° oven for 1 hour. Cool on a rack.

Banana Nut Bread

Another extremely popular baking-soda fruit bread, rich in flavor and rather tight in texture, this is more banana-y than the one that follows. It is extraordinarily good for small sandwiches or as a breakfast or luncheon bread, and it makes excellent toast. The top may crack during baking, but that is of no great consequence.

[1 large loaf]

½ stick (¼ cup) butter
½ cup granulated sugar
½ cup honey
2 eggs
1½ cups mashed, very ripe bananas
  (3 heavy ones should do it)
1½ cups all-purpose flour
½ teaspoon baking soda
½ teaspoon salt
½ cup sliced nuts, almonds or your choice

Cream the butter with a wooden spoon. Add the sugar and honey and beat till creamy and light. Add the eggs, one at a time, then thoroughly mix in the bananas. Sift together the flour, soda, and salt and blend thoroughly into the mixture. Finally fold in the nuts.

Butter a 12 x 4½ x 2½-inch loaf tin and pour in the batter. Bake in a preheated 350° oven 1 hour, or until a knife inserted in the center comes out clean.

Banana Bread

This is another banana bread, which I find lighter and perhaps more flavorful than the previous one, although both are extremely interesting breads. You might experiment and decide for yourself.

[1 loaf]

2 cups sifted all-purpose flour
1 teaspoon baking soda
½ teaspoon salt
½ cup butter or other shortening
1 cup granulated sugar
2 eggs
1 cup mashed, very ripe bananas
   (about 2 bananas)
⅓ cup milk
1 teaspoon lemon juice or vinegar
½ cup chopped nuts

◄⋅ Sift the flour with the soda and salt. Cream the butter and gradually add the sugar. Mix well. Add the eggs and bananas and blend thoroughly. Combine the milk and lemon juice, which will curdle a bit. Slowly and alternately fold in the flour mixture and milk mixture, beginning and ending with the dry ingredients. Blend well after each addition. Stir in the nuts, then pour the batter into a lavishly buttered 9 x 5 x 3-inch pan and bake in a preheated 350° oven for 1 hour, or until the bread springs back when lightly touched in the center.

Prune Bread

Like all fruit breads, this is moist and rather rich and sweet. It is a delicious bread for breakfast or for tea, and it is good for certain types of sandwiches, such as those with fillings of fruit and nuts or olives and nuts. Also, since pork and prunes are complementary, cold pork or ham sandwiches on prune bread make an excellent and novel combination. Be sure to start the prunes marinating the day before you make the bread.

[1 large loaf]

2 eggs
1 cup milk
¼ cup sherry or Madeira, in which
   the prunes have marinated for 24 hours
½ cup granulated sugar
½ teaspoon salt
½ teaspoon ground cinnamon
2 cups all-purpose flour
3 teaspoons double-acting baking powder
1 cup finely chopped prunes, previously
   marinated and drained

Mix the eggs, milk, and sherry or Madeira in a mixing bowl, and sift in the sugar, salt, cinnamon, flour, and baking powder. Stir until well mixed, and finally add the prunes. Pour into a well-buttered bread pan or soufflé dish or any 6-cup mold you choose; a round loaf is rather pleasant in this case.

Bake in a preheated 350° oven for 50 to 60 minutes, or until nicely browned. There will probably be a crack across the top, which is usual with baking-powder breads. Let it cool in the mold for 5 minutes, then turn out and cool on a rack.

With baking powder or soda breads you will notice that very often the bread cracks across the top, although otherwise it gives you a beautiful even crumb and slice. Don't worry! Such breads are wont to break during the baking period because they are usually somewhat heavier. If you find doughy or hard lumps in the slice it is certain that you did not mix the original dough well.

Apricot Bread

Like all of the fruit breads made with baking powder, the apricot loaves are quite rich and have beautiful color and rather tight texture. They also have a wonderful bouquet. Don't be disturbed if the loaves crack slightly in the middle as they bake. This seems to be par for the course.

[2 loaves]

1 cup boiling water
1½ cups (1 package) dried apricots
½ teaspoon baking soda
1 cup granulated sugar
2 eggs
2¾ cups all-purpose flour
3 teaspoons double-acting baking powder
1 cup chopped nuts

◄? Pour the boiling water over the apricots and let stand until just tender; don't oversoak them. Drain off the water and reserve it. (If you don't have 1 cup, add more water to it.) Roughly chop the apricots. Pour the liquid into a large mixing bowl, add the baking soda, sugar, and eggs, and mix well with a wooden spoon. Then add the apricots, flour, baking powder, and nuts and mix well again.

Butter and flour two 9 x 5 x 3-inch loaf tins. Divide the batter into two equal parts and pour into the tins. Bake in a preheated 350° oven for about 45 minutes, or until the breads have risen, are dark in color, and a straw or knife comes out clean when inserted in the center. Cool on racks and serve.

Quick Cranberry Bread

This is an unusually good version of an old American favorite, with a couple of unorthodox variations. The cranberries give the loaf good touches of color and a pleasant tartness.

[1 large loaf]

3 cups all-purpose flour
1 teaspoon baking soda
1 teaspoon double-acting baking powder
1 teaspoon salt
2 eggs
1 cup granulated sugar
¼ cup melted butter
1¼ cups milk mixed with 1 teaspoon rosewater
1¼ cups raw cranberries, cut in half
  or roughly chopped
¾ cup chopped walnuts or pecans

◄ Sift the flour with the soda, baking powder, and salt. In a mixing bowl, by hand or with a beater, beat the eggs and sugar until well blended. Stir in the melted butter and the milk mixed with the rosewater. Stir in the flour just until moistened, and then fold in the cranberries and nuts. (Do not overwork or beat the dough.) Butter a loaf tin about 10 inches long and 4 to 5 inches wide and spread the dough in the tin. Bake in a preheated 350° oven for about 55 to 60 minutes, or until the center of the bread springs back when touched lightly or a cake tester comes out clean when inserted. (The top will often crack, which is typical of soda and baking powder breads.) Let stand in the tin for a few minutes before turning out on a rack to cool. When thoroughly cooled, wrap in plastic or foil and let sit overnight or at least a day before cutting. Store in the refrigerator.

VARIATIONS

• **Cranberry Orange Bread:** Use ½ cup orange juice and ¾ cup milk as liquid in the bread. Add, with the cranberries, 3 tablespoons grated orange rind.

• **Cranberry Sauce Bread:** Instead of raw cranberries and sugar, use 1½ cups cranberry jelly or, preferably, canned whole or unstrained cranberry sauce. Beat the sauce into the eggs as you would beat in sugar. Use only ¾ cup milk or orange juice in the recipe. Add 3 tablespoons orange rind, if you like.

Quick Fruit Bread

This can be made with either candied orange or chopped marinated prunes, or a combination of both. It is another of the quick baking-powder breads that are becoming increasingly popular in this country. The fruit flavor is readily apparent and quite delicious. It is an excellent gift bread, makes pleasant toast, and keeps well.

The top is likely to crack considerably, which is typical of baking-powder breads, and the loaf will not rise very high. When it is turned out the color is golden, with tiny specks of orange visible. A hard outer crust will develop as the bread cools.

[1 loaf]

3 cups all-purpose flour
½ cup granulated sugar
½ teaspoon salt
3 teaspoons double-acting baking powder
1¼ cups milk
1 egg, lightly beaten
6 tablespoons melted butter
1 cup diced candied orange
3 teaspoons orange flower water

Sift the flour, sugar, salt, and baking powder into a mixing bowl. Add the milk and beaten egg and combine thoroughly. Add the melted butter, candied fruit, and orange flower water. Mix well.

Butter a 9 x 5 x 3-inch loaf tin. Pour in the batter and bake in a pre-heated 375° oven 45 to 50 minutes, or until a knife comes out clean.

VARIATIONS

• Double the recipe to make one orange-flavored loaf and one prune loaf. Separate into two batches before adding the fruit and flavoring. Prepare one batch as in the master recipe. To the other batch add ½ cup chopped prunes that have been marinated in Madeira, ½ cup pistachios, and 3 teaspoons rosewater. Proceed with the recipe.

• Add 1 tablespoon caraway seeds to the master recipe.

Raw Apple Bread

A rather unusual baking powder bread that you will find delightfully textured and interesting in color and flavor. It keeps very well and, as a matter of fact, will be better if left to mature for at least 24 hours. It is a fine bread to give as a gift.

[1 large loaf]

> ½ cup butter or margarine
> 1 cup granulated sugar
> 2 eggs
> 2 cups all-purpose flour
> ½ teaspoon salt
> ½ teaspoon baking soda
> 1 teaspoon double-acting baking powder
> 2 tablespoons buttermilk or soured milk
> 1 cup coarsely chopped, unpeeled apples
> ½ cup coarsely chopped walnuts or pecans
> 1 teaspoon vanilla extract or grated lemon rind

Cream the butter or margarine, add the sugar slowly, and continue to beat until light and lemon colored. Beat in the eggs. Sift the flour with the salt, baking soda, and baking powder. Add to the creamed mixture alternately with the milk, beginning and ending with the dry ingredients. Stir in the apples, nuts and vanilla or lemon rind.

Butter a 9 or 10 x 5 x 3-inch loaf tin. Spoon the batter into the tin and bake in a preheated 350° oven 50 to 60 minutes, until the loaf pulls away slightly from the sides of the tin or until a straw or cake tester inserted in the loaf comes out clean. Cool in the pan for about 5 minutes, then loosen from the pan and turn out on a rack to cool completely before slicing.

VARIATION

• Sprinkle about 1 tablespoon chopped nuts on top of the batter before baking.

Pain de Fruits (Fruit Bread)

Interesting in flavor and nicely textured, this French fruit bread is excellent for toast. It bakes to a delicious-looking rich brown and is a very attractive gift bread.

[1 loaf]

4 eggs
½ cup granulated sugar
1⅓ cups all-purpose flour
1½ teaspoons double-acting baking powder
½ teaspoon ground cinnamon
1 teaspoon salt
6 tablespoons butter, melted and
    quickly removed from heat
3 ounces filberts, ground
4 ounces almonds, ground
4 ounces dried figs, cut into small pieces
2 ounces candied citron, diced
½ cup golden seedless raisins, presoaked
    in warm water for 1 hour

❧Line a 9 x 5 x 3-inch bread pan with buttered waxed paper. Beat the eggs and sugar until they form a ribbon. Sift together the flour, baking powder, cinnamon, and salt and add, along with the melted butter, to the eggs and sugar. Then add the nuts, figs, citron, and raisins and blend thoroughly. Pour into the prepared pan and bake in a preheated 350° oven for 50 to 60 minutes. Cool slightly in the pan, then remove the loaf to a rack to finish cooling.

Lemon Bread

This is a tart, deliciously refreshing bread with a character all its own. I had a feeling that lemon flavor in a baking powder bread might work out very well, so I experimented and came up with this. I am delighted with it, and find that it keeps extremely well.

[1 small loaf]

1 stick (½ cup) butter
½ cup granulated sugar
Rind of one lemon, finely chopped or
    coarsely grated
2 eggs
½ cup lemon juice
2 cups all-purpose flour
3 teaspoons double-acting baking powder
1 teaspoon salt

Cream the butter and sugar together, then add the lemon rind and the eggs, one at a time, beating well after each is added. Stir in the lemon juice, then sift in the dry ingredients gradually. Beat well after each addition until you have a light, workable batter. Pour into a buttered and floured 8½ x 4½ x 2½-inch bread pan and bake at 350° for 50 to 60 minutes. Turn out on a rack to cool. Do not slice until the next day. Serve with butter and preserves as a tea bread.

Persimmon Bread

Persimmons grow in many countries of the world, but often, as in France, they are left hanging on the trees. In this country we have learned to appreciate their superb deep-orange color, their shape, and their delicate flavor, and they are becoming increasingly popular. In earlier times they were allowed to ripen on the trees until dead ripe before being eaten raw or used for puddings, cookies, and breads. Nowadays they show up in our markets in a firm state and must be left at room temperature for several days or a week to ripen until they are almost mushy.

This old recipe, sent to me by a dear friend from the Middle West, makes a bread that is almost cakelike in texture. Spread with good fresh butter, it is very pleasant to eat along with a cup of tea or to use for a cream-cheese sandwich. It is unusual, rich, and thoroughly delicious.

Traditionally this bread is baked in four 1-pound buttered and floured coffee cans, but you can use 3- to 4-cup charlotte molds (my preference), round Pyrex dishes, or round stainless steel bowls.

[4 round loaves]

3½ cups sifted all-purpose flour
1½ teaspoons salt
2 teaspoons baking soda
1 teaspoon ground mace
2 to 2½ cups granulated sugar, or to taste
1 cup melted butter
4 eggs, lightly beaten
⅔ cup Cognac or bourbon
2 cups persimmon purée (the pulp of
    about 4 medium, very ripe persimmons
    —not necessary to peel)
2 cups coarsely chopped walnuts (optional)
2 cups raisins (optional)

∾ Sift all five dry ingredients into a mixing bowl. Then make a well in the center and add the melted butter, eggs, Cognac, persimmon purée, and, if you like, the nuts and raisins. Mix the dough until it is quite smooth. Butter and flour four molds, fill them about three-fourths full, and bake for 1 hour at 350°. Cool the loaves in the molds and turn out on a rack.

NOTE
Wrap in foil after cooling if you wish to keep them. They will keep nicely from 1 to 2 weeks.

ROLLS

Parker House   Bread Sticks
Sweet Potato   Alvin Kerr's Zephyr Buns
Crackling Biscuits

Parker House Rolls

Parker House rolls are as much of a tradition in the United States as any bread. They were created, so the story goes, by the Parker House in Boston, which was one of our great nineteenth-century hostelries. They have been copied by every cookbook author and every baker in the country. Some versions are exceedingly good and some are absolutely dreadful because they skimp on good ingredients. Parker House rolls should be delicate, soft, and rather sweet, typical of American rolls in the nineteenth century, and they consume butter by the tons. The dough itself need not be shaped into the classic Parker House foldover. Instead, you can cut the rolled-out dough into triangles and form them into crescent shapes, or you can cut the dough into strips and braid them. There are many other ways to treat this dough, which is very pliable and pleasant to work with.

Parker House rolls freeze well and can be reheated in foil or in a microwave oven. My mother used to make great quantities of them, and they would keep nicely for several days even in the refrigerator, in those days before freezing, and reheat beautifully. They certainly are one of the most delicious rolls I know of.

[About 30 rolls]

2 packages active dry yeast
1 tablespoon granulated sugar (see note below)
½ cup warm water (100° to 115°, approximately)
½ stick (¼ cup) butter, cut into small pieces
2 cups warm milk
5 to 6 cups all-purpose flour
2 teaspoons salt
¼ to ½ cup melted butter
1 egg, beaten with 2 tablespoons light cream or milk

Dissolve the yeast and the sugar in the warm water and allow to proof. Melt the ½ stick butter in the warm milk, then combine with the yeast mixture in a large mixing bowl. Mix 2 to 3 cups of flour with the salt and stir, 1 cup at a time, into the mixture in the bowl, beating vigorously with a wooden spoon to make a soft sponge. (The dough will be wet and sticky.) Cover the bowl with plastic wrap, set in a warm place, and let the dough rise till doubled in bulk, about 1 hour. Stir it down with a wooden spoon and add about 2 more cups of flour, 1 cup at a time, to make a dough that can be kneaded with ease. Turn out on a lightly floured board and knead until velvety smooth and very elastic; press with the fingers to see if the dough is resilient. Let rest for a few minutes, then form the dough into a ball. Put into a buttered bowl and turn so that the surface is thoroughly covered with butter. Cover and put in a warm, draft-free place to rise again until doubled in bulk.

Punch the dough down with your fist, turn out on a lightly floured board, and let rest for several minutes, until you are able to roll it out to a

Parker House cut and folded

thickness of ½ inch. Cut out rounds of dough with a round 2- or 2½-inch cutter, or with a water glass dipped in flour. (The odd bits of leftover dough can be reworked into a ball, rolled out, and cut.) Brush the center of each round with melted butter. Take a pencil, a chopstick, or any cylinder of similar size and make a deep indentation in the center of the circle, without breaking through the dough. Fold over one-third of each round and press down to seal. Arrange these folded rolls on a buttered baking sheet about ½ inch apart. Brush again with melted butter and allow the rolls to rise until almost doubled in size. They will probably touch each other. Brush them with the egg wash and bake in a preheated 375° oven until lightly browned, about 20 minutes, depending on size. Test one by gently tapping it on the top. If done, you will hear a very faint hollow sound. Or take one, break it open carefully, and see if it is cooked inside.

Remove the rolls to a cooling rack or serve piping hot right from the oven, with plenty of butter and preserves or honey, if desired.

NOTE
The original recipe calls for 2 tablespoons sugar; however, I feel that the rolls are richer in flavor if the sugar content is reduced.

VARIATIONS
• The dough can be rolled out and cut into triangles and shaped into crescents. Roll from the wide end of the triangle to the point, first brushing with water, then bend the ends in a bit. Brush with an egg wash and sprinkle with sesame seeds or poppy seeds. Arrange on a buttered baking sheet and allow to rise and bake in the same way as the standard rolls.

• The dough can also be made into little braided rolls; or it can be rolled into tiny balls and placed, in groups of threes, in well-buttered muffin tins. In either case, allow the rolls to rise, brush them well with the egg wash, and bake as directed for Parker House rolls.

cloverleaf

butterflakes

• **Butter Flakes or Butterfly Rolls:** Roll dough on a floured surface into a rectangle 9 x 14 x ¼ inches. Brush with melted butter and cut into five strips about 9 x 1¼ x ¼ inches each. Stack and cut into 1½-inch stacks. Place stacks, brushed with butter, cut side down, into buttered muffin tins. Follow directions above for rising and baking.

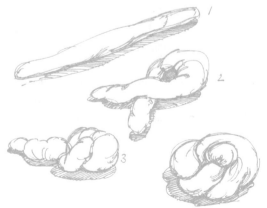

• **Twists:** Roll small pieces of dough into 9-inch strips. They should be approximately ½ to ⅔ inch in diameter. Tie in loose knots and place on buttered cookie sheets. Let rise and bake according to directions above.

Sweet Potato Rolls or Bread

This is a traditional American bread that can also be made with winter squash. It is deep yellow in color and has lightness and a lasting moisture. It is probably better baked as rolls than as a loaf; however, either form comes through extremely well.

[About 24 rolls or 2 loaves]

2 packages active dry yeast
4 tablespoons granulated sugar
½ cup warm water (100° to 115°, approximately)
3 tablespoons melted butter
1 tablespoon salt
3 eggs
3 to 3½ cups all-purpose flour, approximately
½ cup mashed sweet potatoes or yams
    (if canned, drained of all liquids first)
2 tablespoons cream

◄⅜Combine the yeast with 1 tablespoon of the sugar and the warm water in a mixing bowl and let proof for 5 minutes. Add the remaining sugar, the butter, salt, and 2 of the eggs to the yeast mixture, and stir to blend well. Stir in the flour, 1 cup at a time, then stir in the sweet potatoes. Turn out on a lightly floured board and knead for 2 or 3 minutes, adding only enough flour to prevent the dough from sticking to the board. (The dough will be soft, so do not knead too heavily.) When the dough is smooth and springy to the touch, shape it into a ball. Put in a buttered bowl and turn to coat the surface with butter. Cover with plastic wrap and let sit in a warm, draft-free spot until doubled in bulk, about 1 hour.

Punch the dough down, then shape it into a ball and let rest for 2 minutes. Pull off equal pieces about the size of golf balls and shape into balls—about 2 dozen of them. Place them on a buttered cookie sheet about 2 inches apart or, if you want the rolls joined, about ¼ inch apart. Cover and let rise until doubled in bulk. Beat the remaining egg with the cream and brush this onto the rolls. Bake in a preheated 375° oven for about 20 minutes, or until the rolls sound hollow when tapped on the bottom and are a lovely brown color.

VARIATION

• After the dough has had its first rising, punch down, let rest for 2 minutes, and then turn out on a floured board. Divide in half, shape into loaves and place in two buttered 9 x 5 x 3-inch loaf pans. Let rise until almost doubled in bulk. Bake at 375° for 40 to 45 minutes.

Bread Sticks

Bread sticks can be made in many different ways. For example, you can use ordinary bread dough, roll it into pencil-thin cylinders, and bake on a sheet sprinkled with cornmeal; or you can use Parker House roll dough (page 186), roll it into very, very thin cylinders, and bake without a preliminary rising on a buttered sheet sprinkled with cornmeal. The baking time is about 15 minutes at 375°, or until the sticks are browned.

Other types of bread sticks, like those done here, are given a slight rising after being shaped, and if they are allowed to rise still further, they make small loaves or what the French call *baguettes*, similar to French bread and pleasant to eat fresh or even warm. The bread sticks made from this dough taste yeasty and have a nice crunch to them. They will keep well for several days and are fun to serve with salads, as a snack with drinks, or with first courses.

[About 20 sticks]

2 packages active dry yeast
1 tablespoon granulated sugar
2 teaspoons salt
¼ cup olive oil
1½ cups warm water (100° to 115°, approximately)
3 to 3½ cups all-purpose flour
1 egg white beaten with 1 tablespoon water
Coarse salt, sesame seeds, poppy seeds (optional)

◀◗In a large mixing bowl combine the yeast, sugar, and salt. Add the oil and ¼ cup of the water. Beat this mixture well with a wooden spoon for about 3 minutes. Add ½ cup of the flour and continue beating with the wooden spoon. Alternately add flour, 1 cup at a time, and water until you have a fairly soft dough, reserving approximately ½ cup flour for kneading. Remove the dough to a floured surface, and knead for several minutes until it springs back very briskly when you press your fingers in. It must be smooth and satiny, and all the flour on the board should be absorbed.

Let the dough rest on the board, covered with a towel, for about 5 minutes, then shape it into a roll about 20 to 22 inches long. With a very sharp

knife cut it into at least 20 equal pieces. Rest the dough again for 3 or 4 minutes, then, using the palms of your hands, roll out each piece as long as the baking sheet or sheets you will use. (Or roll them any size you like and cut them.) Oil or butter the baking sheet, sprinkle lightly with sesame or poppy seeds, and arrange the bread sticks on it about 1 inch apart. Let them sit about 20 minutes, until they just barely begin to rise. Just before putting them in the oven, brush them lightly with the egg and water mixture and sprinkle with coarse salt, sesame seeds, or poppy seeds. Bake in a slow oven (300°) for about 30 minutes, depending upon the size of the bread sticks. They should be nicely browned and very crisp.

NOTE

These will stay crisp for several days, stored in an airtight container.

VARIATIONS

• To make *baguette* loaves, let the lengths of dough rise longer, or until they have doubled in bulk. Slash them with a sharp knife or a razor blade, brush with the egg wash, and sprinkle with coarse salt, sesame seeds, or poppy seeds. Bake as above; they will take about 40 to 45 minutes.

• To make twisted breadsticks, roll out as directed above. Using two hands, pick up the rolls and twist, turning clockwise with one hand, counterclockwise with the other. Return to baking sheets and bake as directed above.

Alvin Kerr's Zephyr Buns

These buns have beautiful texture, shape, and color, perfect for an elegant dinner or luncheon.

[18 buns]

1 package active dry yeast
2 tablespoons warm water (100° to 115°, approximately)
2 tablespoons granulated sugar
1 teaspoon salt
3 eggs
2 cups sifted all-purpose flour
¼ cup melted butter
1 teaspoon cool water

Soften the yeast in warm water and stir in the sugar and salt to dissolve. In a bowl, beat 2 of the eggs and blend in the flour. Then stir in the yeast mixture and melted butter. Knead vigorously in the bowl with the hands, till the dough leaves the sides of the bowl and is elastic—about 5 minutes. Make into a ball, put in a buttered bowl, and cover with plastic wrap. Let rise in a warm, draft-free place for 1½ hours, or till doubled in bulk. Punch down and divide into 18 equal pieces. Roll the pieces into balls and arrange, well separated, on a buttered baking sheet. Let rise 30 minutes, or until doubled in size. Brush with the remaining egg beaten with a teaspoon of water. Bake in a preheated oven at 375° for 10 minutes, or until nicely browned. Cool on a rack.

Crackling Biscuits

Crackling bread, found in many countries, has always been one of the more novel breads. It was a way of using the crisp residue from rendering pork or goose fat. In Italy a dough like the Pizza Caccia Nanza on page 60 is often braided into a rough loaf, with very coarsely ground black pepper and cracklings added. In America we've been cooking cracklings in both white bread and cornbread for a long time. Here I am going to give you an unusual Central European crackling biscuit that comes from George Lang's excellent *The Cuisine of Hungary*, perfect for a goulash or a choucroute.

[About 12 to 14 biscuits]

1 package active dry yeast
3 tablespoons warm milk (100° to 115°, approximately)
3¾ cups all-purpose flour, preferably unbleached
1 egg
½ pound pork cracklings, finely chopped
1 tablespoon rum
1 tablespoon salt
1 teaspoon coarsely ground black
    pepper, or to taste
¼ pound melted lard
⅓ cup dry white wine
1 egg yolk, beaten with 1 teaspoon water

◄ Dissolve the yeast in the warm milk and stir in 1 tablespoon of the flour. Let proof for about 10 minutes. Mix the remaining flour with the egg, cracklings, rum, salt, pepper, melted lard, and wine. Thoroughly combine with the yeast mixture, turn out on a floured board, and knead extremely well. Place in a buttered bowl and turn to coat the surface with butter. Cover and let rise in a warm, draft-free spot until doubled in bulk, about 1 hour.

Punch the dough down, and let rest for 3 or 4 minutes, then roll out, fold over, and cover with a cloth. Let rest again for 10 minutes. Repeat this process three times, rolling, folding, and resting. After the final rest period, roll out the dough to a thickness of ½ inch and cut into rounds 1½ inches in diameter or into squares. Score the tops of the biscuits in a lattice pattern with a very sharp knife and brush with the beaten egg yolk. Let the biscuits rest until the glaze dries, then place on buttered baking sheets and bake in a preheated 400° oven about 25 minutes.

FLAT BREADS

Pita   Norwegian Flatbread
Armenian Thin   Lefse

Pita Bread

Pita bread is that flat, round, softish bread called, among other names, Syrian bread, Armenian bread, and Middle Eastern bread. Its two layers are almost separated in the baking, and one can split it very easily to use with shish kebab and even with hamburgers, as well as all kinds of other sandwiches. It is also extremely good buttered, cut into strips, and baked in a slow oven to get quite crisp, to be served like Melba toast with soup or salads or cold fish dishes. It can be wrapped and stored in the refrigerator or frozen successfully.

Pita bread must not be allowed to get crisp when it comes freshly baked from the oven, but should be wrapped in foil or plastic to keep the bread loose and soft after the puffing up that occurs during baking. Although it can be made with all-purpose flour, it's much better made with hard-wheat flour, which gives a better texture and rises better. Pita loaves are great fun to make.

[8 or 9 round loaves]

2 packages active dry yeast
¼ teaspoon granulated sugar
2 cups warm water (100° to 115°, approximately)
¼ cup olive oil
1½ tablespoons salt
6 cups hard-wheat flour, approximately
Cornmeal

◄? Dissolve the yeast and sugar in ½ cup warm water in a large mixing bowl and allow to proof. Then add the remaining 1½ cups water, along with the oil, salt, and 5 cups flour, mixing in vigorously, 1 cup at a time. (The dough will be rather sticky.) Turn out on a floured board and work in the remaining cup of flour or more if the dough is too sticky. Knead for a good 10 minutes or more until the dough is smooth and elastic. Shape into a ball, place in a buttered bowl, and turn to coat with butter on all sides. Cover and let rise in a warm, draft-free place for 1½ to 2 hours, or until doubled in bulk.

Punch down the dough, turn out on a floured board, and allow to rest for 10 minutes. Divide into eight or nine equal pieces and shape each piece into a ball. Cover the balls with a cloth or foil and let rest for 30 minutes. Flatten each ball with a well-floured rolling pin and roll to ⅛-inch thickness in approximately 8-inch circles. Dust two baking sheets with cornmeal, place two circles on each sheet, cover, and let rest again for 30 minutes. (Leave the four remaining circles on a lightly floured working surface and transfer them to the baking sheets, dusted again with cornmeal, when the first four are baked.)

Preheat the oven to 500°. Put one of the baking sheets on the lowest rack of the oven for 5 minutes. *Do not open the oven door until the 5 minutes are up!* Transfer the sheet to a higher shelf and continue baking 3 to 5 minutes longer until the loaves are puffed like balloons and just very lightly browned. Repeat the procedure with the second baking sheet, unless, of course, you have a large enough oven so that the baking sheets can go in side by side on the same shelf (or use two ovens, if you are fortunate enough to have two). Remove to prevent a crisp crust from forming and to ensure the familiar spongy pita texture. The loaves should deflate on cooling.

NOTE

After cooling, the pita can be frozen. The loaves will reheat in the oven in 10 to 15 minutes.

Armenian Thin Bread

Throughout the Middle East one finds many versions of the crisp flatbreads. The one I have chosen here is simple to make, a good keeper, and extremely pleasant in flavor and texture. It is also a nicely accommodating bread that seems to go along with almost any type of food. I find it keeps best in a tightly covered tin.

[4 10 x 14 sheets]

1 cup warm water (100° to 115°, approximately)
1 package active dry yeast
½ stick (¼ cup) butter or margarine, melted and cooled to
*   lukewarm*
1½ teaspoons salt
1 teaspoon granulated sugar
3¼ to 3¾ cups all-purpose flour

◄ Pour the warm water into a large, warm bowl, sprinkle in the yeast, and stir until dissolved. After it has proofed, add the cooled butter, salt, sugar, and 2 cups flour. Beat until smooth. Add enough additional flour to make a stiff dough. Turn out onto a lightly floured board and knead until smooth and elastic, about 8 to 10 minutes. Place in a buttered bowl and turn to coat with the butter. Cover and let rise in a warm spot until doubled in bulk.

Punch the dough down, divide into four equal pieces, and roll each piece into a rectangle 10 x 14 inches. Place on ungreased baking sheets and bake in a preheated 350° oven about 20 minutes, or until golden brown. Remove from the sheets and cool on racks. If desired, the bread can be softened by holding under running water. Serve with cheese or other appetizers.

Norwegian Flatbread

You are probably familiar with the packaged thin, crisp flatbread from Norway. Often used for pâtés or spreads it is extremely popular all through the country. This delicate commercial bread has been made for centuries at home and is not difficult to prepare. It entails a deft rolling job, but is well worth the trouble because of the crisp, mealy flavor that is excellent with smoked fish or salt meats cut paper thin.

[4 12-inch rounds]

2 cups coarse barley flour
2 cups coarse whole-wheat flour
1 teaspoon salt
1 to 1½ cups lukewarm water

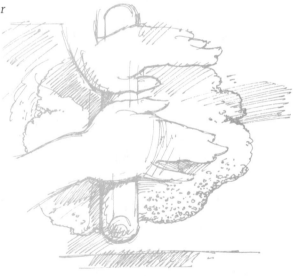

Blend the flours and salt and gradually stir in the water until the dough pulls away from the sides of the bowl. Transfer to a floured board and knead thoroughly. Divide the dough into four parts and roll into paper-thin circles about 12 inches in diameter or to fit your griddle —or an iron skillet will do. Lightly flour the griddle and bake the dough over rather low heat. (Pierce the dough lightly with a fork before placing it on the griddle if you wish to keep it from bubbling.) It will take 15 to 18 minutes for each side; the bread must be extremely crisp.

NOTE
The flatbread may be stored in a large wooden box or in a tin.

Lefse

Lefse is a rather unusual flatbread of Scandinavian origin, and there are many different recipes for it. It can be eaten warm or cold. When cold it grows quite firm and crisp, but is traditionally dipped lightly into water and softened before being rolled with a filling or simply spread with butter. When it is eaten warm, it should be taken from the griddle, folded into a napkin, and served with butter, cheeses, preserves, or other fillings. In either case, it is easy to prepare and delightful to eat.

[12 to 14 *lefse*]

1 cup sour milk or buttermilk
¼ cup granulated sugar
6 tablespoons corn syrup
½ teaspoon baking soda
⅛ teaspoon cardamom
3½ cups all-purpose flour, approximately

Combine the ingredients and work the mixture with the hands, or in an electric mixer with a dough hook, to make a soft, pliable dough. Divide the dough into two pieces and roll each piece about ⅛ inch thick into a square, oblong, or circle. Cut into squares or circles with a 4- or 6-inch cutter. Bake on a lightly floured griddle, over quite low heat, 12 to 15 minutes on each side. The *lefse* should color very slightly.

NOTE

If it is not to be eaten warm, *lefse* should be stored in a tin or a box, where it will become crisp.

FILLED BREADS

Pissaladière   Pizza Loaf
Lahma bi Ajeen

Pissaladière

This is one form of the Provençal version of pizza. It calls for tomatoes, puréed onions, anchovies, and ripe olives and is baked using a brioche dough or a plain white bread dough. I prefer the brioche. Use the recipe for Brioche Bread (page 147), flattening the dough out into a wide pan and spreading the filling over it. It makes an attractive, delicious hors d'oeuvre or luncheon dish. I used to buy it in a bakery in St. Rémy in Provence, where I lived several summers, and found it much to my liking, as I am sure you will.

[8 to 12 servings]

1 recipe brioche dough (see Brioche Bread, page 147)
6 large ripe tomatoes or 1 one-pound can
    Italian plum tomatoes plus
    2 tablespoons tomato paste
Olive oil
1 or 2 cloves garlic, peeled
    and crushed
3 medium Spanish onions
3 tablespoons butter
Freshly grated Parmesan cheese
½ teaspoon rosemary, crushed
    in a mortar
Anchovy fillets
Ripe olives, preferably the soft
    Italian or Greek type

◄ Prepare the brioche dough. While the dough is rising, prepare the filling:

Peel, seed, and cut the tomatoes in very small pieces (or, if using canned tomatoes, drain, seed, and chop). Heat 2 tablespoons olive oil in a skillet, add the tomatoes and garlic, and let them reduce to a paste over medium heat, stirring occasionally. Peel and chop the onions and steam them in the butter over low heat, covered, until they form a rather thick purée.

After the first rising, roll the dough out to about ⅜ inch in thickness and line two 9-inch-square cake tins or one 12-inch tart pan. Brush with softened butter and put in a warm place to rise slightly.

Sprinkle the brioche shell with the grated Parmesan. Spread the onions over it, and sprinkle with the rosemary. Cover with the tomato purée. Arrange the anchovies in a lattice pattern on the tomatoes, and place an olive in the center of each opening. Brush the olives with a little olive oil. Bake in a preheated oven at 375°, until the crust is golden and cooked through, about 25 to 30 minutes. Brush the top with more olive oil before serving hot as an hors d'oeuvre or a main luncheon dish.

Pizza Loaf

This is a rolled loaf that I often bake in a soufflé mold. I have a glass mold that is perfect for it, although porcelain works well too. The loaf has great flavor and texture and is made with a filling reminiscent of pizza. It is ordinarily served warm as a first course for an Italian meal or as a cocktail snack. Extraordinarily good in a novel way, it does not keep very well, and should be made only if it can be eaten still warm from the oven.

[12 servings]

1 package active dry yeast
1 teaspoon granulated sugar
1½ cups warm water (100° to 115°, approximately)
1 tablespoon salt
3 tablespoons olive oil
3½ cups flour, preferably hard-wheat
3 to 4 tablespoons of a very spicy
    tomato or pizza sauce
½ teaspoon dried basil
½ cup freshly grated Parmesan cheese
½ cup freshly grated mozzarella cheese
1 egg white, lightly beaten with 1 tablespoon water

◄৫ In a mixing bowl combine the yeast, sugar, and ½ cup of the water, and allow the yeast to proof. Add the rest of the warm water to the yeast mixture along with the salt and the olive oil. Stir in the flour and beat with a wooden spoon or with your hands to make a stiff, sticky dough. Turn the dough out on a well-floured board and knead until velvety smooth and elastic but firm, about 10 minutes. Oil a large bowl, add the dough, and turn to thoroughly coat with the oil. Place in a warm, draft-free spot to rise until about doubled in bulk, 1 to 1½ hours.

Punch the dough down, turn out on a lightly floured board, and let rest for 4 or 5 minutes, or until you can roll it out easily. Roll into a rectangle about 7 inches wide and 15 inches long. Spread with the sauce—

a homemade, well-spiced tomato sauce or a prepared pizza sauce that has some flavor and distinction (I would not recommend catsup or chili sauce), leaving an inch of border on all sides. Sprinkle with the basil, Parmesan cheese, and mozzarella, and starting from the wide end, roll in jelly-roll fashion. Pinch the edges well, form into a circle, and fit into a buttered 6- to 8-cup mold. (Be sure it is tightly rolled and well sealed, so the sauce does not ooze out during baking.)

Brush the roll well with the egg wash and place in a warm, draft-free spot to rise until doubled in bulk. (A thorough rising is very important here.) Meanwhile, preheat the oven to 400°. Place the mold on the middle rack of the oven and bake for 20 minutes, then lower the temperature of the oven to 350° and continue to bake another 35 to 45 minutes, or until the bread sounds hollow when you remove it from the mold and rap it, top and bottom, with your knuckles.

Let cool in the mold for 5 to 10 minutes, then remove to a rack. Serve warm, cut into wedges.

NOTE

For a higher glaze, brush the loaf with an egg wash about 10 minutes before it leaves the oven.

Lahma bi Ajeen

A flat loaf topped with a mixture of lamb, pine nuts, tomato, and garlic, this Arab counterpart of pizza is exceedingly delicious, intriguing looking, and a delightful change from other dishes of this type. It makes a nice snack for lunch, or it can be cut into small pieces and served with cocktails. What's more, it is fun to make.

[8 servings]

FOR THE DOUGH:

1 package active dry yeast
Pinch of granulated sugar
Scant 1 cup warm water (100° to 115°, approximately)
1 pound all-purpose flour (about 3¾ cups)
1 teaspoon salt
2 tablespoons olive oil

FOR THE FILLING:

1 pound finely chopped onion
Olive oil
2 cloves garlic, peeled and finely minced
1½ pounds finely ground shoulder of lamb
½ cup pine nuts

½ six-ounce can tomato paste
1 teaspoon granulated sugar
¾ teaspoon ground allspice
1 tablespoon lemon juice
4 teaspoons salt, or to taste
1 teaspoon cracked peppercorns
2 dashes of Tabasco sauce
3 tablespoons chopped parsley

To prepare the dough, dissolve the yeast, with the sugar, in about ½ cup of the lukewarm water and allow to proof for about 10 minutes. Put the flour and salt in a large, warm mixing bowl. Make a well in the center and add the oil and the yeast mixture. Work the dough vigorously, adding the remaining lukewarm water gradually to make a soft dough. Knead, in the bowl, for about 15 minutes, until the dough is pliable and elastic. Cover with a damp cloth and set aside in a warm place for 2 to 3 hours, or until doubled in bulk. Lightly oil the top of the dough to prevent a crust from forming.

Meanwhile, prepare the filling. Sauté the onions in 1 tablespoon olive oil until wilted but not browned. Remove from the heat and add garlic. Add to the ground meat along with the rest of the ingredients and blend well. Make a small sample patty, fry in ½ teaspoon olive oil, and taste. Correct the seasonings. Set aside while you roll out the dough.

Turn out the dough on a lightly floured board and knead a few times. Divide into walnut-sized balls and allow to rest for a few minutes, then roll each piece with a lightly floured rolling pin into a circle 5 to

6 inches in diameter. Spread the prepared filling generously over each piece. Transfer each piece after you have prepared it to a lightly oiled baking sheet. Bake in a preheated oven at 450° to 500° for 8 to 10 minutes. The patties should be well done but still pale in color.

FRIED CAKES

Raised Doughnuts   Cake Doughnuts
Maple Bars   Dough Gobs
Buñuelos

Raised Doughnuts

These are old American standards and remain hearty, delicious tidbits for breakfast or for picnics or just between-meal snacking. The filled ones have long been great favorites of mine. They will keep very well if frozen when fresh; reconstitute them in an oven at 350° for 15 minutes or in a microwave oven for 1½ minutes.

[About 12 to 14 doughnuts]

½ package active dry yeast
2 tablespoons warm water (100° to 115°, approximately)
½ cup granulated sugar
1 egg
1 cup warm milk or ½ cup evaporated milk
    plus ½ cup warm water
2 tablespoons melted butter or margarine
3¾ cups sifted all-purpose flour
    (about 1 pound)
Lard, shortening, or cooking oil
    for deep frying
Confectioners' sugar or additional
    granulated sugar (optional)
½ teaspoon salt

Place the yeast in a mixing bowl, add the warm water, and stir. Add the sugar and mix well. Let stand 10 or 15 minutes to proof. With the hands or 2 wooden spoons, stir in the egg, then the milk, melted butter, flour, and salt. Continue to stir until the dough is springy. Brush the top of the dough lightly with additional melted butter or margarine and cover with waxed paper or foil. Place in a warm, draft-free spot to rise until doubled in bulk, about 1½ hours. (Note, however, that this dough is easier to roll out if put in the refrigerator to rise overnight, or at least for 4 hours.)

Punch down and turn out on a floured board. Roll out half the dough at a time to a thickness of about ½ inch. Cut with a floured doughnut cutter and place on a board or waxed paper-covered cookie sheet to rise until doubled in bulk.

Heat 2 or more inches of lard, shortening, or cooking oil to 370° in a large frying kettle or an electric skillet. Put the doughnuts in, a few at a time, top sides down. Fry until brown on one side, then turn to brown on the other side. When nicely browned, remove from the hot fat and drain on absorbent paper. (Check to maintain the temperature of the fat at 370° for every batch. If too low, the doughnuts will absorb fat and be soggy.) Sprinkle with con-

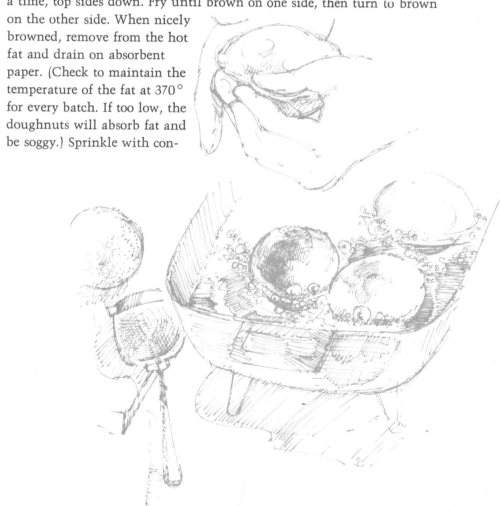

fectioners' sugar or granulated sugar, if desired, while still warm. (The easiest way to attain an even sugaring of the doughnuts is to put the sugar in a large plastic or paper bag and gently shake a few at a time in the bag.)

VARIATIONS
• **Filled Doughnuts:** Filled doughnuts, jelly doughnuts, or "cannon balls" were long famous throughout Central Europe before they became part of American cookery.

Prepare the basic recipe for raised doughnuts. After the dough has been allowed to rise once, punch it down and roll out on a lightly floured board to a thickness of about ¼ inch. Cut into rounds 3 or 4 inches in diameter—no holes in these—and place ½ teaspoon jam, jelly, or pastry cream on the centers of half of the rounds. Brush the edges with 1 egg lightly beaten with 2 tablespoons water. Place the other half of the rounds over the filled ones and press the edges together gently. Transfer to a board or cookie sheet and allow to rise until almost doubled in bulk. Fry as for the doughnuts in the master recipe, in deep fat heated to 370°.

• For a richer dough use 3 egg yolks instead of the whole egg. A plain white bread dough can also be used.

Maple Bars

Maple bars are one of my great weaknesses, and I must confess that even now when I go to a bakery and see those luscious rectangles of fried dough with a maple glaze on them I am tempted to indulge and usually do. They are a delightful American invention.

[About 12 bars]

◄ To prepare, use the recipe for Raised Doughnuts (page 212). After the dough has risen, punch it down and roll it out in a square or rectangle about ½ inch thick. Cut it in pieces about 2 inches wide and 4 to 5 inches long and set them on a board to rise until amost doubled in bulk. Then drop them, a very few at a time, into deep fat at 370° and let them brown very nicely on both sides. Remove them from the fat and let them drain on absorbent paper. Spread one side with a maple glaze made with ¼ cup of maple syrup mixed with 1 cup confectioners' sugar; or you can mix 2 or 3 tablespoons hot water with 1 cup sugar and ⅛ teaspoon maple flavoring.

Cake Doughnuts

These fried cakes, which originated in New England, have been overwhelmingly popular in the American diet. Those of you who hark back to World War I will remember that the Salvation Army established itself in history with girls who carried doughnuts through to the trenches. People gave money for doughnut machines so they could be turned out by the thousands for the troops. Nowadays cake doughnuts are covered with chocolate and all kinds of icings, which are sometimes revolting. Simply sprinkled with granulated or confectioners' sugar they can be a toothsome morsel, and the holes are even more so. In fact, fried doughnut holes are one of my favorite dishes. Cake doughnuts are trouble to make because the dough must be kept chilled and one must work with several batches. So they do take a little time—but they are worth it.

[About 18 doughnuts and holes]

1 cup granulated sugar
½ stick (¼ cup) butter
2 eggs
4 cups sifted all-purpose flour
1 tablespoon double-acting baking powder
1 teaspoon salt
½ teaspoon ground mace
¾ cup milk
Corn oil or vegetable shortening for deep frying
Confectioners' sugar, additional granulated sugar,
   or cinnamon sugar

◄ Cream the sugar and butter together in a bowl very, very well, and then beat in the eggs, one at a time. (I like to work with my hands on this.) Then combine the dry ingredients and gradually add to the creamed mixture, alternately adding the milk. When the dough has reached a nice consistency, cover the bowl and chill it in the refrigerator for two hours. Remove from the refrigerator and take out one-quarter of the dough.

Start heating the fat to 370°; an electric skillet is very good for frying doughnuts because you can regulate the heat easily. Roll the dough out to a thickness of ¼ inch on a floured board. (If you want thicker doughnuts roll to ½ inch.) Cut with a doughnut cutter, or with a round cutter and a smaller cutter to take out the center. When the fat has reached 370° fry two or three doughnuts at a time, or as many as will fit comfortably into the pan. As soon as one rises to the surface turn it with a wooden spatula or a pair of tongs. When nicely browned on both sides remove from the fat and drain on absorbent paper. Sprinkle with confectioners' sugar, granulated sugar, or cinnamon sugar. (Then fry the holes. They puff up and are delicious.) Take another quarter of the dough from the refrigerator, and continue until you have used up all the dough; or you can fry only part of the dough, if you like, and refrigerate the remainder to fry at a later time.

Dough Gobs or Fried Dough

Dough gobs are an old American food that dates back to the time when every household produced bread regularly. A housewife put her bread to rise overnight and in the morning took a piece of the risen dough, punched it down, rolled it out, cut it into odd shapes, and dropped the pieces into hot fat to cook until golden brown on all sides. These "gobs" were served with syrup, honey, or preserves and sometimes with bacon and eggs and proved to be a crisp, delicious breakfast dish. On Nantucket there used to be, and may still be for all I know, a summer hotel where on Wednesdays, Fridays, and Sundays one could go and have dough gobs for breakfast. They were simply marvelous.

To prepare dough gobs use any of the white bread recipes or the Raised Doughnuts (page 212). Roll out some of the risen dough, cut it into any shapes you want, or just take chunks, pat them down, and drop them into fat heated to 360° to 365°. Cook them until brown and crisp, and serve them with plenty of maple syrup and good bacon or ham.

Buñuelos

Similar forms of this deep-fried pastry are found in Europe and in Latin America. In France they are known as *galettes à l'huile,* and in Italy, where they are shaped into bow knots, they are called *farfallette dolci.* Paper-thin and crisp, they are absolutely marvelous when sprinkled well with cinnamon and confectioners' sugar. Sometimes they are made into a dessert by adding a cream or a syrup to them. This version comes from Mexico.

[About 36 pastries]

1 teaspoon salt
2 tablespoons granulated sugar
4 cups all-purpose flour
1 teaspoon double-acting baking powder
2 eggs
1 cup milk
¼ cup melted butter
Oil for deep frying
Confectioners' sugar
Cinnamon (optional)

Sift all the dry ingredients together. Beat the eggs thoroughly and then beat the milk into the eggs. Gradually combine the egg-milk mixture and the dry ingredients, and finally add the melted butter. Turn out on a floured board and knead until quite smooth and elastic. (I then like to divide the dough into about 36 tiny balls and roll them out individually, but you can roll out the dough and cut it into 4- to 6-inch rounds or squares.) Fry the pieces in deep fat heated to about 370°. When done they will curl somewhat and become golden brown and crispy. Drain well on absorbent paper, and sprinkle with confectioners' sugar and cinnamon or just with confectioners' sugar. Serve as a cookie.

GRIDDLE BREADS

Girdle Scones

Among the breads baked on a griddle (the Scots insist on saying "girdle"), scones seem to run high in popularity. They are rather sour-flavored because of the buttermilk content, and their delicate texture makes them excellent when hot, split, buttered well, and spread with raspberry jam. Cold, they are best cut in half, toasted, and served swimming in butter. Exceptionally easy to make, they are apt to be a novelty to some people.

[8 to 12 scones]

2 cups all-purpose flour
1 teaspoon cream of tartar
½ teaspoon salt
1 teaspoon granulated sugar
1 teaspoon baking soda
Buttermilk or sour cream

◄ Sift the flour, cream of tartar, salt, sugar, and baking soda together. Take a cupful of the mixture and combine it with enough buttermilk or sour cream to make a soft dough. Pat it with the hand on a floured board and form into a circle ½ inch thick. Cut in wedges and bake on a floured griddle over a medium heat until lightly browned, then turn to brown on the other side. Serve hot or cold.

Scones formed
and cut in quarters

Potato Scones

Potato scones are paper-thin, rather odd in flavor, and extremely interesting. They are usually served cold with sweet butter, but there is no reason why they can't be offered warm, wrapped in a napkin. They have a kinship to some forms of the Scandinavian *lefse*.

[18 scones]

1 cup warm mashed potatoes
⅓ cup melted butter
1 teaspoon salt
½ cup sifted all-purpose flour

◄᠎᠎Mix the mashed potatoes, butter, salt, and flour until thoroughly blended. Divide the dough into thirds and roll out each third into a circle about ¼ inch thick. Cut each circle into sixths and bake on a hot floured griddle, or in a hot floured skillet, for about 5 minutes, turning once to cook on both sides.

Crumpets

Crumpets bear a close similarity to English muffins and to English muffin bread. Rather soggy and holey, they must be toasted and treated to quantities of butter and good homemade jam. They were formerly standard tea food in England, but have for some reason lost their popularity. I still love them, maybe because of the buttery heaviness.

Crumpets are baked in rings on a hot griddle. You can use small flan rings available in kitchen equipment shops, or failing that, you can use empty 7-ounce cans, such as those in which salmon and tuna come packed, with both the top and bottom smoothly removed.

[8 to 10 crumpets]

½ cup milk
½ cup boiling water
1 package active dry yeast
1 teaspoon granulated sugar
1½ teaspoons salt
1¾ cups sifted all-purpose flour
¼ teaspoon baking soda, dissolved in 1 tablespoon hot water

◄⅔Combine the milk and boiling water and cool to lukewarm. Add the yeast and sugar and allow to proof. Blend the salt and the sifted flour, combine with the yeast mixture, and beat thoroughly for several minutes with a wooden spoon or with your hand. Let the batter rise in a warm place until almost doubled in bulk and rather bubbly. Add the dissolved soda and beat into the batter. Allow to rise again until doubled in bulk.

Spoon the batter into buttered rings placed on a moderately hot griddle to a depth of about ½ inch. Cook until dry and bubbly on top. Remove the rings, turn the crumpets, and brown lightly on the other side. Let cool. To serve, toast and flood with butter.

Yeast Griddle Cakes or Pancakes

These are simply wheat-flour pancakes made with a starter. In earlier times people kept a starter going especially for pancakes. Nowadays we usually make the starter the night before, which is what we are doing in this case. It makes light, puffy, absolutely delicious pancakes.

[About 12 to 14 cakes]

1 package active dry yeast
1 cup warm water (100° to 115°, approximately)
2 to 3 tablespoons granulated sugar
2 cups all-purpose flour
1 egg
½ teaspoon salt
3 tablespoons melted butter
1 cup evaporated or fresh milk

The night before making the pancakes combine the yeast, water, 1 tablespoon sugar, and 1 cup of flour in a mixing bowl. Cover with a cloth and leave overnight to rise. The next morning beat the egg well in a mixing bowl and add 1 to 2 tablespoons sugar. Beat again, add the yeast mixture, and stir in the salt, butter, and the second cup of flour; add milk if mixture seems too thick. However, the batter *should* be a little thicker than is customary. The pancakes should be baked on a well-buttered griddle. Serve at once with melted butter, syrup, or honey, and bacon, ham, or even a little steak.

Yeast Buckwheat Cakes

Buckwheat cakes have had a strong part in American cookery for the last 150 to 200 years, epitomizing the hearty fare of country life. The batter would be left to rise overnight, then in the morning the cakes were mixed and baked and served spanking hot for breakfast with good slices of country ham, bacon, or sausages and sometimes with all three, as well as with maple syrup, honey, or treacle, and tons of butter.

[About 20 small pancakes]

> 1 package active dry yeast
> 2 cups warm water (100° to 115°, approximately)
> 1 teaspoon salt
> 1 cup all-purpose flour
> 1 cup buckwheat flour
> 2 tablespoons molasses
> ¼ teaspoon baking soda
> 1 tablespoon melted butter

The night before, mix the yeast with the water in a large bowl, add the salt and the flours, and cover the bowl with a cloth. Let the batter stand all night in a warm place. In the morning, add the molasses, baking soda, and melted butter to make a very, very thin batter. Bake on a well-buttered griddle two or three cakes at a time, and serve them on a hot plate with plenty of melted butter and warm syrup or honey.

NOTE

If you want to perpetuate the starter for future use: Dissolve a package of yeast in 3 cups lukewarm water. Add 1 teaspoon salt and 1 cup each of white and buckwheat flour. The next morning take out 1½ cups of the starter and add ¾ cup warm milk, 2 tablespoons molasses, ¼ teaspoon soda, 1 tablespoon melted butter, and another ¾ cup white flour and ¾ cup buckwheat flour. Proceed to bake as described in the master recipe. Cover the remaining starter loosely and refrigerate. The night before using, again add 1 cup lukewarm water, 1 teaspoon salt, and 1 cup each of the flours, and in the morning proceed as described in the beginning of the Note. Again store the starter. This will work for quite some time if you renew the starter frequently.

Index

additives, 5–7
all-purpose flour, 2–5
almonds
  in banana nut bread, 170
  in Kugelhopf, 130–1
  in *pain de fruits,* 180
  in raisin and nut bread, 112–13
Alvin Kerr's zephyr buns, 194
Anadama bread, 101
anchovies
  in *pissaladière,* 204–5
aniseed
  in Swedish limpa, 128–9
apple bread, raw, 179
apricot
  bread, 175
  glaze for rich sour-cream coffee
    cake, 118–20
Armenian
  bread, 198–9
  thin bread, 200

baguette(s), 192–3
  loaves, 193
baking soda, 8
  see also soda breads
baking powder, 8
baking powder bread(s) and biscuits
  apple, raw, 179
  apricot, 175
  baking and mixing of, 174
  biscuits, 160–1
    cream, 162
  Carl Gohs' zucchini, 169
  Clay's cornsticks, 167
  cranberry
    orange, 177
    quick, 176–7
    sauce, 177
  fruit, quick, 178
  Helen Evans Brown's corn chili, 166
  lemon, 181
  pain de fruits, 180
  prune, 172–3

banana
  bread, 171
  nut bread, 170
barley flour, 5
  in Norwegian flatbread, 201
barley meal, 5
bars, maple, 215
basic home-style bread, 36
basic white bread, 22–35
basic yeast bread and other white-flour
    breads, 21–72
basil
  in pizza loaf, 206–7
batter bread(s), 149–57
  dill-seed, 155
  English muffin, 156
    for microwave oven, 157
  golden cake, 154
  Sally Lunn, 152–3
Bavarian rye bread, 102–3
beer
  in Finnish sour rye bread, 92–3
  in *verterkake,* 132–3
biscuits
  baking powder, 160–1
  crackling, 195–6
black bread, 104–5
Boston brown bread, 168
Bourbon
  in persimmon bread, 182–3
bowls, how to grease, 12
bran, 5
brandy
  in rich sour-cream coffee cake, 118–20
bread(s)
  for afternoon tea or coffee, 19
  basic white, 22–35
  for breakfast, 17
  and butter, 15–16
  cooling, 13
  croutons, 17
  crumbs, 17
  defects, suggestions for remedying,
    33–5

A NOTE ABOUT THE AUTHOR

James Beard was born in Portland, Oregon, in 1903, and it was there that his palate was educated at an early age. His first cookbook, *Hors d'Oeuvre and Canapés*, was published in 1930. After that he wrote nineteen other books on food, including *The James Beard Cookbook*, for years a best-selling paperback; the much-honored *James Beard's American Cookery*; and the companion volumes *Theory & Practice of Good Cooking*, which explored all the whys and wherefores of cooking as he taught his students, and *The New James Beard*, which put into practice what he preached. However, it is his highly popular *Beard on Bread* that has been his best-selling book of all time.

He started giving cooking lessons in the late 1950s, in what later became the kitchen of the famous restaurant Lutèce. This was the beginning of his popular cooking school, later located in his own brownstone in Greenwich Village, which now houses the James Beard Foundation. Well known throughout the country, James Beard traveled extensively and taught and demonstrated cooking nationwide. He died in New York in 1984.